AF512204

Alternative Education

Alternative Education

Philosophy, Curriculum and System

Bindhu C M

SHIPRA

All rights reserved. No part of this publication may be reproduced or transmitted, in any form or by any means, without prior permission of the copyright holder and publisher.

The opinions and views expressed in this book are of the author(s) own and hence should not necessarily be attributed to the institution where s/he is employed and s/he is solely responsible for plagiarism & copyright issues, if any that arises.

₹ 850
US$ 34
ISBN: 978-93-91978-29-7

First Published in India in 2022

Alternative Education:
Philosophy, Curriculum and System

© Prof. Bindhu C M

Published by:
SHIPRA PUBLICATIONS
LG 18-19, Pankaj Central Market
I.P. Ext., Patparganj, Delhi 110092, India
Tel.: +91 11 2223 5152/6152; 96500 28065
E-mail: info@shiprapublication.com
www.shiprapublication.com

Dedicated to

My Beloved Husband

Late Dr. P. K Sudheesh Kumar

Faculty of Education, Calicut University

Who is a never ending source of inspiration in my academic career and in my whole life.

Contents

1

Alternative Education

Concept, Components and Approaches

Concept

Alternative Education, as a school programme, is maintained and operated by a local or regional board of education. It is offered to students in a non-traditional educational setting and helps to address the social, emotional, behavioural and academic needs of the students. Alternative education is different from that of formal and conventional education system and its basic structure is related to the needs and interests of the students. Students enrolled in alternative education are those whose needs are not met in the traditional system of education.

Therefore, alternative education must be set up in such a way that it is responsive to the needs of students by offering different programmes, variety of experiences and unconventional timings. Due to this, different types of teaching and learning methods, approaches and techniques are used in alternative education. Hence, different types of opportunities are provided by alternative education in all stages of education, both at school level and at higher education level. The problem of inaccessibility of higher education by a large group of learners is addressed by implementing such systems in alternative education. They will surely reinforce the desire and confidence in such learners.

Besides giving academic rigour and cultural relevance of instruction, alternative education supports students beyond mere graduation, by building positive relationships, enhancing student's strengths, talents, behavioural and socio-emotional needs. Alternative education may function within a single school or it can be a programme affiliated with one or more schools or even districts. It covers a wide variety of educational activities which fall inside and may be even outside the system of formal education. Needless to add, alternative education is available at different levels of education which include elementary, secondary, senior secondary and higher education levels. Even though alternative education works within a well prescribed curriculum, it is very much flexible in approach. It does not stick on to any kind of rigid admission procedures, time bounded teaching-learning approaches, examination patterns, classroom setting etc.

Common Features among Alternative Education World Over

A major problem related to alternative education is the lack of any standard definition on various forms of alternative education. Globally alternative education differs in its definition and application. So, generalisations are difficult. However, there are many common features among alternative education practised in other parts of the world.

- Evaluation and enrolment have clearly defined goals
- Wholehearted implementation by avoiding a piecemeal approach to structuring programmes
- Autonomy
- Student-centered approach
- Good integrated approach in research as well as practices in main areas such as assessment, curriculum, teacher competencies and integration of special education services
- Training and support for teachers who work with risk populations with or without disabilities
- Links to multiple agencies that may become increasingly important as alternatives are required to serve students with special education needs
- Enrolment of choice as against school-determined placement.

The uses of alternative education can be understood in multiple ways in India based on the ways in which it is offered to those who are willing to use it. Many states and institutions offer it but in different names and different ways. Some of these are:

- Bridge course centres which prepare children for formal schooling
- Centres established for some specific, difficult groups of *out of school* children for mainstreaming or otherwise
- Centres under Alternative Innovation Education (AIE) component of the Education Guarantee Scheme (EGS).

Alternative Innovation Education (AIE) centres can be considered as temporary hostels for children who migrate. They provide condensed or abridged courses or sometimes back to school camps for the mainstreaming of out of school children. This is attempted to achieve competencies which are appropriate for their age. They are also of a short period in nature like residential camps or drop in centres for street and slum children. Schools which are set up in unserved habitations under EGS and AIE scheme try to give good education to children who went out of school. These alternative schools are known by different names in different states. For example, in Kerala it is known as Multi-grade Learning Centres. The courses which are conducted in such centres are common alternative forms for out of school children and migrating children, which aim at mainstreaming them in formal schools. The centres are residential and temporary. The children are prepared there for admission in specified classes so that they can be absorbed into formal government recognised schools. Therefore, in Indian context, one may easily assert that alternative education offers educational opportunities to aspirants who have discontinued their education at some stage due to certain reasons. It is also clear that there is no prescribed or standard definition for the term.

Need

Even though we have a number of facilities for the educational development of the people, majority of students do not have access to these facilities. A study conducted by UNICEF reveals that a large number of students have been dropped out from formal government schools due to unfavourable impression of school. And the study also reflects that most of the SC/ST students and their parents opined that higher caste and rich families are only the beneficiaries of education. The children, who are never enrolled in schools, have parents with no education or lower level of education. Prof. Yampa committee reported that some students refused to compromise with non-comprehensibility of education and they preferred to drop out rather than wasting years in rote learning, without knowing the value of education. However, some scholars said that they felt some constraints related to poor physical facilities and quality of education and another reason for dropout was failure to pass the examinations. One point that has to be kept in mind is that relevant curriculum content and good physical facilities should motivate students to complete their education and utilise their schooling to attain a good quality life.

The need for alternative education can be related to India's struggle for achieving universalisation of elementary education. It is not possible because we do not have enough schools. Socio-economic reality of our country is the major challenge in achieving this target. Not only that, the enrolment in existing schools is very low which stands as a challenge in the allotment of new schools. The crucial reason behind low enrolment is that, in most of such families children work in the fields with their parents. In some cases elder ones have to act as baby sitters for younger ones, if their mother works for wages or have to take other household responsibilities. Considering these situations, the educational system conceived the system of Non-formal Education in 1978 to meet the requirements of those children who are unable to attend formal schools. This process was meant to be a part of micro-planning strategy, to reach out to every family and every child and involve them in the process of education. But flexibility, localisation and need of specific strategies have often been used as loopholes to offer low quality education through Non-formal Education.

In India, the existing educational conditions and facilities do not suit to many people. The true benefits of education do not reach the masses. So education system in India requires an expansion of the school system and with inclusion of Non-formal Education system, it may be set right. Attempts are to be made to find an educational paradigm under Alternative School.

Alternative School is a system which has a delivery mechanism distinct from formal schools and non-formal education. Alternative School has been conceived as transacting the same curriculum and textual materials as in the formal system but outside the main structure of education system. It is essentially the degree of flexibility in curriculum design and teaching-learning approach that makes the difference between the formal and the alternative schools.

Scope

Education plays a great role in every person's life. But some of them have not got any opportunities to attain education. Alternative education acts as a blessing for these categories of people and this helps them find a way to achieve the educational goals of the society. Alternative education programmes focus on what they can offer to the students, and not on the problems student faced in his previous education programme. Alternative education is a vital component of the total educational system. The term alternative made some confusion in some people; it mainly focuses on differently abled students, rather than being for the education of all children and often for adults as well. Sometimes it is useful to distinguish educational options for the developmental needs and learning styles of the children.

Alternative education institutions are not rigid with rules and procedures. It avoids many school bureaucratic cultures and remains flexible with warm learning atmosphere. Each alternative institution creates and maintains its own teaching-learning methods and approaches. Each alternative approach is based upon slightly, and sometimes drastically different beliefs about what it means to live, learn, love and grow in today's society.

Aims and Objectives of Alternative Education

Aims

Effective implementation of alternative education helps to address the children from different rational and ethnic groups and those with special needs. States and communities are increasingly turning their attention to alternative education for promoting it into the main stream of public education system. Most of the traditional schools have adopted the activities and education approaches that alternative schools pioneered. The main aims of alternative education are:

1. To liberate access to things by abolishing the control which persons and institutions now exercise over their educational values.
2. To liberate the sharing of skills by guaranteeing freedom to teach or exercise them on request.
3. To liberate the critical and creative resources of people by returning to individual persons the ability to call and hold meetings now

increasingly monopolised by institutions which claim to speak for the people.

4. To liberate the individual from the obligations to shape his expectations to the services offended by an established profession by providing him the opportunity to draw on the experience of his peers and to entrust himself to the teacher, guide, advisor or healer of his choice. Inevitably, the alternative education society will blur the distinction between economics, education and politics on which the stability of the present world order and the stability of the nations now rest.

Objectives

Due to different reasons, people discontinue their education. Alternative education enables them to continue it. But while continuing the discontinued education as before, they prefer to attain certain personal and professional capabilities and basic life skills. The main objectives of alternative education are:

- Provide access to available resources for all who wish to learn, regardless of their age.
- Empower all who are willing to share what they know by finding those who wish to learn.
- Furnish all who wish to present an issue to the public with opportunity to make their challenge known.
- To develop the ability to understand their environment better and shape it powerfully with their own hands.
- To develop inter communication skills for the alternative use of technology.
- To give reference services to educational objectives, this would liberate and enable everyone to access it.
- Open and free individual skill exchange, for the establishment of relational structures throughout the society.
- Independent educators will be replaced with the school teachers
- To ensure that all citizens have equal share in educational resources.
- To develop free and independent thinkers to live in a democratic society.

Components of Alternative Education

Community Service Learning: Alternative education students need opportunities to prove their worth as citizens and as individuals. Alternative students can move toward improving their lives and the environment that sustain them. The students use their abilities and skills for the benefits and progress of the society.

Intensive Academic Monitoring: The population of alternative schools is risk students (having more probability of failing academically due to their cicumstances) as they have never gone to schools, dropouts, sickness, employed and repeaters etc. They have had some problems with regular schools. So they need individual care and intensive academic monitoring.

Partnership with local college/university (Community colleges): There is no need of exclusive place for conducting alternative education programme. It can be conducted in regular schools and college premises, in their off times. Thus alternative education programme shares the facilities of the regular schools or colleges.

Small group learners (Small teacher-pupil ratio): In alternative concept, each student needs specific attention to develop their skills. The small-sized schools with unique characteristics bring children and teachers together, wherein children get personalised attention with a wide range of choices in subjects. The teacher-student ratio will range from 8-25 students per teacher, as successful efforts have an average ratio of 1:16.

Parent/family Involvement: Parent and family have a major role in alternative education. Apart from alternative education teachers, parents also take care. So they should volunteer to keep time of the programme and also participate in family life seminars.

Life Skill Training: Because of their inabilities and living conditions, most of the alternative education learners face adjustment problems with societies. Life skill training provides students with training in personal self-management, social skills and resistance skills which are necessary for living in a society.

Conflict Resolution Training: Some of the alternative education learners sometimes show emotional instability. The disagreement may be personal, educational or social. So they need a training to resolve the disagreement.

Partnership with Community based Organisations: Coordination is the objective of these community-based organisations. Whatever is happening in the community should be taught in the schools and whatever is taught in the schools should happen in the community. Besides this, other citizens of the community should be brought to schools for purposeful programmes and the students of the schools should be taken into the community for execution of appropriate tasks. Thus, the problems of school and community are solved jointly by all students, teachers and other people. It is beneficial for both community and school.

Work based Learning Opportunities: Work based learning provides students with opportunities to study complex subject matter as well as vital workplace skills in a hands-on. Work based learning supports students in the work place, as also those who are in part time employment.

Flexible schedule for Academic Instruction: The alternative education learners are special categories like disabled, working people, aged, dropouts, etc. So they need flexibility in time schedule, content and academic instruction.

Factors Leading to Alternative Education

There are four factors that lead students to alternative education programme. Each student may be led to alternative education due to one or all of these factors. The factors are student related, family related, school related and community related. Each factor is described below.

Student related Factors

Each student has unique character and they face so many problems based on these characters. These things force them to dropout from their previous school.

- Attendance/truancy
- Behaviour/Discipline problems
- Pregnancy/Parenting
- Drug abuse
- Poor peer relationship
- Suspension/expulsion
- Illness/disability.

Family related Factors

Sometimes family problems and situation may compel students to drop out from their schooling.

- Low socio-economic status
- Dysfunctional home life
- Low parental involvement
- Low parental expectations
- Domestic violence
- Low language proficiency.

School related Factors

As the students have to spend majority of their active time in schools, some factors related to school may contribute to the increasing rate of dropouts.

- Conflict between home and school culture
- Ineffective discipline system
- Lack of adequate counselling
- Negative school climate
- Lack of relevant curriculum
- Passive instructional strategies
- Inappropriate use of technology
- Disregard of student learning style
- Suspension/expulsion
- Low expectations
- Lack of language for instruction/communication.

Community related Factors

The community in which the students live has a significant role in setting conducive environment for their study. The following community related factors may also accelerate dropout process.

- Lack of community support service
- Lack of community support for school
- High incidence of criminal activity
- Lack of school-community linkage
- Lack of public transportation
- High mobility/homelessness.

Specific Populations in Alternative Education

Education provides an individual not only a healthier and positive outlook towards everything in life but it also enables him/her to earn a livelihood. Unfortunately, a lot of students end their education in midway due to known and unknown reasons. It leaves an impact on their personal and professional lives. The society faces its consequences. One obvious consequence is that the society will be compelled to provide long-term support to such individuals. Here, the concept of alternative education comes handy. It helps to provide education for such school dropouts. Alternative school also helps high risk, special education students too. They may be placed in alternative schools due to the difficulties they face in adjusting and absorbing themselves in our typical conventional classroom settings. For some of them, counselling services too are used to build better coping skills.

Some specific categories of populations who are subjected to Alternative Schools are:

1. Dropouts

There are so many reasons for drop out, mainly from school related and family related factors. Poor academic achievement, school environment, school size, relation with teachers, relation with peers, teaching-learning strategies, curriculum, classroom ecology are the major school factors leading to drop out.

The percentage of dropouts depends upon student's socioe-conomic status as well as the educational level of parents. Children may be the victims of family dysfunction issues such as neglect, caregivers facing addiction issues or other family members dropping out of school. Other considerations start from the support the students get from their families in issues related with personal safety in the community or at home. Other issues related with child care, involvement in criminal cases even incarceration seems to be other reasons for drop out from school. In other cases, psychiatric issues and long-term hospitalisations may also lead to drop out. A student's sudden reaction to frustration and failure in school serves as a way to define different types of dropouts. They are:

- *Quiet dropouts*: They are low achieving students who experience failure over a period of time, and therefore, simply walk away from school when they attain the age to legally do so.
- *Disruptive dropouts*: They are low achieving students who act out their frustration at lack of school success. These students are often suspended for long periods of time or are expelled from the public school classroom and are labelled push outs.
- *High academic achievers*: They are considered pushouts because they leave out of boredom as well as out of resistance to rigid school rules.
- *In-school dropouts*: These are students perceived to be non-achievers or minimal achievers without acting out behaviours.

2. Students with Disabilities

Students who require special education and related services are another specific population thought to benefit from alternative education. Though generally alternative schools are not specifically designed to serve students with disabilities, many students who have been identified as requiring special education or related services attend alternative schools and programmes. Students with emotional behavioural issues or learning disabilities often struggle in the conventional school system and they may become disenfranchised and drop out for many of the same reasons as their non-disabled peers. In fact, the dropout rates of students with disabilities are more than those without disabilities. Researches in the early 1990's shows that the dropout rate of students with disabilities are 20 per cent higher than the students of the normal school population. So, students of special education may feel less confident with years of learning frustration, finding it easier to quit rather than keep struggling. They often face some struggle with conventional school system and also with non-disabled peers. Associated with this frustration, behaviour becomes less consistent and life choices made from that point of view can produce negative outcomes. Many of the aspects of alternative programmes that may make them appropriate to serve students with disabilities. These aspects are small school size and individualised instruction.

3. Students with High-risk Behaviours

One of the major elements that many students bring to the alternative setting is a set of high-risk behaviours. These students places themselves at serious risk by participating behaviour such as drug use, drunk driving, unprotected sex, suicide attempts, weapon use, gang involvement, criminal activity engagement etc. These behaviours stem out from poor self esteem and they fail to return to school.

Philosophical Bases of Alternative Education

Philosophy of alternative education is different from conventional educational philosophy in many important ways. The main difference is based on psychological components. For example, in traditional education, we believe that individual and his/her interpersonal growth as a condition for the development of intelligence and the enhancement of goals of learning. At-risk students want an atmosphere to satisfy their unique needs for safety, trust and recovery from their past failure. Based on these, the philosophy of alternative education must be well founded in psychological theory and sound educational practices.

It is instructive to examine the difference between the philosophy of the alternative school movement and the philosophy of the traditional epistemological approach. Our conventional school pedagogy is given more importance to academically driven process and is subject centered. Based on these activities they chart the daily routine schedule. The outcome of the process is evaluated by using standardised measures.

Epistemological philosophy fails to address the requirements of at-risk students and reiterates their exclusion by improper acknowledgment of the psychological needs. The mismatch so created between the school's purpose and the necessities of at-risk students leads to a form of cultural reproduction. Theory of Cultural reproduction states that groups or social classes show a tendency to develop systems that reinforce the power and position that those groups do hold. It is clear that in the case of schools, success is assessed by grades, advanced placements etc. These achievements are the product of having the cultural capital to thrive within that system. Some examples of cultural capital are vocabulary, homework and personal experience. Schools analytically devalue the cultural capital of students who occupy subordinate class positions. A student devoid of any tools for success, like a strong and supportive family is at a big disadvantage. In cultural reproduction theory, such students are already marked to repeat the failures which they continuously face in the background they are coming from.

Philosophically, the pedagogy for at-risk students must be essentially diverse from the epistemological basis of regular system of education. It is important that alternative schools have to work in a holistic fashion. This is to induce the best relevant practices of mental health, education and systems. Through them they have to build programmes that attend the needs of the youth they address and serve. It is of much importance that the philosophy of alternative school must echo a much profound consideration about the necessities of the student apart from his/her family as a system of human resources. Due to this reason, philosophy of alternative education is best structured in such a way that it is primarily psychological in nature. This relates also to the philosophical paradigms of existentialism apart from phenomenology. The thrust is primarily upon the individual and his or her development as an authentic self. To achieve end, all the processes of the school has to reflect a positive evaluation of the student and his/her culture. The emphasis needs to remain on the dignity and respect of the student and his/her family in daily instruction. This approach of the new alternative school helps to build a positive relationship between the student, his/her family and the school personnel. This relationship is ultimate in signifying the school's desire to include in an educational experience those who have got previously excluded.

The success of a student who undergoes alternative education is clearly rooted in his/her capacity to consider and see himself as a capable and lovable individual. Only from such a positive attitude of self-acceptance of him/her and his/her culture, a healthy and successful relationship with society, school etc. can be built. To be successful with at-risk students, it is also of significant importance that they establish a good personal relationship with their teacher. Many a time, it is because of a good relationship with the teacher that alternative education students find out a personal reason to study. Such a relationship is very much similar to the one that an individual develops with a mentor. The teacher must also understand that the habits of students deeply contribute to their failure patterns. All these understandings and measures taken to rectify the problems and challenges caused by them help the teachers to reach out to these students and teach them well.

To break the strong chains of habits and also to develop routines that help one to be successful in school, a significant paradigm shift has to occur within alternative education students. To develop new habits and belief systems, they have to take efforts to avoid and drop their old and problematic ones. Only after such changes, they will be able to create confidence and trust in their teachers. The philosophy of alternative education welcomes the necessities of an individual in their journey for self-knowledge and acceptance. Needless to add, only from that abode of internal peace and congruence we will be able to produce a worthy citizen who is ready to participate and contribute in a good democratic community.

Various Forms of Alternative Education

Levels of education can be divided into three — primary, secondary and higher education. A wide category of educational alternatives is available at these levels. These are:

1. ***Choice based School:*** School is the first place where students acquire knowledge. The remaining part of education is based on this foundation. If it is strong, the life will be safe. Choice based school is a programme that allows students to choose to attend any private and public schools. They usually select the school based on a system of vouchers, tax credits, scholarships etc. Actually, these programmes are intended to give parents more input in which primary and secondary schools their children attend. This creates competition among schools

for education. The competitive spirit enables parents to select a school that provides better instruction, strong discipline, better academics and life skills.

2. ***Alternative School:*** When the educational programmes and curriculum follow non-conventional method, it is known as an alternative school. These schools offer very flexible programmes with a special curriculum. And they also have a wide range of philosophies and teaching methods. Some alternative schools have strong political, scholarly or philosophical orientations, while others are more ad-hoc assemblies of teachers and students dissatisfied with some aspect of mainstream education.
3. ***Independent School:*** Independent schools function without any external support. These schools do not receive any financial assistance from national or local government. It is operated by tuition fees, gifts from persons and also from endowment funds. Independent schools follow democratic principles and enjoy more autonomy in educational practices and approaches. They have freedom to construct their own curriculum, transaction methods and even the selection and appointment of teachers.
4. ***Umbrella School:*** An umbrella school is an alternative education school that serves to oversee the home schooling of children to fulfil government educational requirements. Umbrella schools are varying in what they offer and the cost. Some of them offer group classes with a defined curriculum, sports, field trips, standardised evaluation systems and more. While others exist only to meet the minimum legal requirements, allowing parents to choose their curriculum, teaching-learning strategies as well as the evaluation systems.
5. ***Home based Education:*** When students get education from parents, guardians or sometimes by home tuition rather than in a public or private school education, it is known as home based education. Home schooling can be an option for families living in isolated rural areas. This schooling is opted by parents those who are living abroad temporarily and those who travel for job purposes constantly. Home schooling is a legal option for parents who wish to provide their children a different learning environment from the one that exists in nearby schools. Some families select home based education on religious grounds. Home schoolers often take advantage of educational opportunities at museums, libraries, community centres, athletic clubs, after school programmes, science preserves, parks and other community resources. Students at secondary level have the option to attend the classes in community colleges which typically have open admission policies. Home schooling also refers to instruction at home under the supervision of umbrella schools.

6. ***Charter Schools:*** A charter school is a public school that functions as semi autonomous unit. It is not allowed to charge. Its charter is a document, an agreement of rules, legislation, curriculum, that is periodically evaluated to see if it has the objectives set in the charter. Charter schools hold the promise of creating a new kind of publicly funded school. It breaks the traditional mould in an effort to help children to achieve at higher levels. This programme enables teachers, parents, community leaders and institutions of higher learning to take the lead in designing public schools that will provide unique and innovative approaches toward achievement in high academic standards.
7. ***Magnet Schools:*** Magnet schools are public schools with specialised courses or curricula. Magnet schools emerged in the United States in the 1960's. Magnet refers to how the school draws students from across the normal boundaries defined by authorities as school zones that feed into certain schools. There are magnet schools at every stage of school education, elementary, middle and high school levels. These schools mainly attract students to particular themes, such as performing arts, farming, animal breeding, etc. Most magnet schools concentrate on a particular discipline or area of study while others have a more general focus. Magnet programmes may focus on academics such as mathematics, sciences, social sciences, humanities and engineering or may focus on technical, vocational or agricultural education.
8. ***Contract Schools:*** School districts 'contract' with an organisation or group to provide public education services. This is the school to teach disruptive and suspended students, programmes to supplement reading services and, in some cases, actually contracting out the entire administrative and educational operation of a school district.
9. ***Correctional Education:*** Correctional education is conducted by resource centres. In this system, children get enrolled and have access to school resources and facilities including an educator for guidance and support. These centres function for 5-6 days in a week. Correctional education gives a platform for discussion to students to critically examine and analyse, through exposure to books, articles and new items.
10. ***Accelerated Learning Programme:*** This programme caters to older boys and girls who have dropped out from school due to war, social and economic problems. They are enabled to be enrolled in regular schools. Similar regular schools' programmes such as curriculum and facilities and classroom settings are used in ALP. This is a four-level programme and at the end of the fourth level, the students get prepared to write final examinations together with pupils in primary to eighth grade and a certificate is awarded to the qualified candidates. They join

formal secondary schools and vocational training institutions. ALP is complimentary to primary education where learners cover the eight years of primary grades in four years.

11. ***Community Schools:*** In this programme community identifies people in their locality who have qualified grade IX and XII. These community members assist in teaching drop outs in the community. The funds for maintenance of community teachers are mainly through contributions from the community. Some communities have started income generated ventures like poultry animal and agriculture farming to raise income of teachers. The role of the government is to provide teaching learning materials and small grants to purchase the learning materials for learners. Some communities give free stay for teachers to attract them into community schools. These schools in farther locations also act as feeder schools to a bigger formal school.
12. ***Interactive Radio Centres:*** Interactive Radio centres by Education broadcasting Services act as alternative approach to primary or basic schooling. A radio is provided to a community school. It provides sufficient opportunities to pupils to learn outside the classroom environment. A teacher is a guide here and facilitates preparation of the lesson for the day at a particular time in advance. The learners are mainly out of school children and those in remote country side locations. They follow instructions given on the radio at a given time. The programme has been useful and the pupils in these classes have proved and shown that learning is taking place.
13. ***Area Learning Centres:*** Area learning centres are open from early morning to late evening year round serving K 12 students and adults. Some other centres are open twenty four hours. The centres offer both General Education Development and regular diplomas as child care available to students on a full or part time basis.
14. ***Blending High School with Colleges:*** A number of states encourage high school students to begin taking college courses during XI and XII grades. Some states created middle colleges within community colleges and universities to better serve high school students. A number of states permit students to double list mutually approved courses so that they meet both high school and college requirements.
15. ***Internet Courses and Programmes:*** During the late 1990's a growing number of courses, programmes and schools available through the internet emerged. These learning opportunities are offered by community colleges, universities, private educational organisations and an increasing number of public school districts.
16. ***Residential Alternatives:*** A number of states in America established academic focused residential science/ mathematics school for gifted and talented students in cooperation with state universities.

17. ***Open Enrolment Programmes:*** Parents and their children may choose to attend any public school in their district or in another district to which their state education funds would follow. Transportation is usually provided if the student's home residence district share a common physical boundary
18. ***Career and Technical Education Programmes:*** CTE programmes combine academic and career readiness to prepare students to be prepared for college and career. Students can receive CTE instruction either within a comprehensive high school or at a designated CTE centre or technical school. CTE participation increases graduation rates for at-risk students and improves post secondary employment and earning outcomes.
19. ***Dropout prevention and Credit Recovery Schools:*** Schools that focus on dropout prevention are often referred collectively to as alternative schools and considered separately from charter, magnet and CTE schools and centres vary widely in purpose, student sub groups served, curriculum and setting. While some alternative schools may aim to prepare students to return to their regular schools, many provide a permanent alternative route to graduation. Alternative school models support students who are at risk of dropping out from residential school, summer school, second chance school and early college high school.

Alternative Education School Models

There developed many schools of choice offering alternative schooling those have been successfully evaluated and replicated. Within these schools exists a wide array of approaches to implementing curriculum, instruction and school governance and management.

1. ***Schools that focus on unique curricular and instructional approaches:*** These schools include: Montessori Schools, based on the idea of Italian physician and educator Maria Montessori; Open schools, outgrowths of the British infant school design; Waldorf schools, inspired by the philosophy of the German educator Rudolf Steiner; Multiple intelligence School founded on based on the theory of Howard Gardner; Paideia schools, established by the philosopher Mortimer Alder; Free Schools and self-directed education based on the concept of the Scottish educator Alexander S Neill; Continuous Progress Schools; Schools without walls; and traditional 'back-to-basic' schools.
2. ***Schools that focus on the needs and interests of students:*** Majority of the schools were developed to address the specific needs of the children. These alternatives include: Teen parent schools, drop out and dropout prevention schools, schools for expelled or incarcerated students and schools for the gifted and talent.

3. ***Schools that focus on career themes and professional relevance:***Career theme magnet schools complement academic studies with intensive experience in work place career settings. These schools which operate primarily at the secondary level, include performing arts schools' radio and television broadcasting schools, health professional schools, law/legal schools, science/ technology schools, teaching career schools, and many other careers focused educational options as well as academic, disciplinary focused programmes in international studies, multi-cultural issues, environmental studies and most of the traditional academic disciplines.
4. ***Schools that focus on experiential learning:*** It is based on the philosophy of John Dewey, learning by doing. These programmes are schools without walls, where students learn in banks, business, courtrooms, museums and government agencies rather than in typical school classrooms. Foxfire, where students learn by collecting and publishing the folklore of their region and Outward Bound/ Expeditionary learning, where students learn through expedition and experiences in their communities.
5. ***Schools that focus on administration, governance and funding:*** There are also numbers of established models for organising, administering, governing and funding alternative schooling. These include the stand-alone alternative schools, schools within walls, clusters of alternative schools and complex system of alternatives.
6. ***School-within-a-school programme:*** School within a school programme may serve a variety of students, including those with emotional and behavioural issues and who are at risk of not graduating. A school within a school programme is unit or learning community within a traditional school that focuses on a particular learning area or style. Students participating in a school within in a school may take classes only in the programme or in addition to mainstream classes. Districts may deliver CTE through a school within a school model rather than a separate site model which may provide increased access and convenience. Career academics are a common type of school-within-a-school programme originally intended to support high school students who are at risk of dropping out. Career academics may have a positive effect on completing high school and raise future earnings and may increase the livelihood of completing college required course work.
7. ***Resource Programmes:*** Students may also participate in an alternative education programme based on a resource room. This programme model parallels the special education "pull out" model where students receive support in an individual or small group setting for part of the day in a separate room. Programmes based on resource rooms may address a variety of student's cognitive, behavioural and social needs and they provide counselling support too.

Key Aspects of Alternative Schools

Many alternative schools have been reflective endeavours that have attempted to deepen and broaden the understanding of the quality of education for all, regardless of different socio- economic backgrounds. Most of these centres, over two decades of hard work behind them, and some institutions have gone back to pre-independence times. The key aspects that characterise these centres are discussed below.

- Non-competitive learning environment: Learning is based on cooperation helping each other and working with each other. Children are not pitted against each other but are encouraged to do their best. Children are allowed to learn at their own pace, avoiding stress and there is an emphasis given to understanding.
- Contextually adapted curriculum: The curriculum is flexible and responsive to the needs and contexts of the learners. The knowledge that children bring from the local cultures, is a part of and often the starting point of the curriculum. The immediate environment is often used as a rich resource for extending learning in the classroom.
- Multilingual environment: Classrooms in many alternative schools have a flexible approach in the use of language. More languages than just the medium of instruction are allowed and used in the classroom. Efforts are made to include the home language of the learner as far as feasible. This facility caters to the better understanding and adjustment of an unfamiliar setting and also enriches the learning process. This helps children from migrant populations and children from homes which use non-standard dialects to settle and adjust better to the school.
- Non-comparative assessment: Assessment in alternative schools is continuous and non-judgmental. Assessment provides teachers with the necessary input to know where the learner is and to adapt and extend the teaching accordingly. Assessment is done in a variety of ways and not only in the form of marks and ranks that compare learners with each other and judge them.
- Flexible pace of learning and transaction of curriculum: The pace of completion of syllabus is planned but not pre-determined or rigid. The learner's ability and capacity are the central factors in determining the pace of teaching. It allows the children in a particular class or teaching group to proceed at different paces and be at different levels in the same subject.
- Inclusiveness: Selection for admission is neither based simply on scholastic achievement nor on ability to pay the fee. Some alternative schools, catering for the weaker sections of society, give free education for their students or provide subsidies for those who cannot afford the regular fees. In a number of the alternative schools

as many as 60 per cent of the children will be supported in this way. A number of alternative schools have been able to include children from different socio-economic backgrounds and special educational needs. Particularly in rural areas there are limited facilities to cater to the children with learning disabilities and so such children often do not receive the special attention and support they need within the framework of the mainstream school. Some of these schools make it a point to take in and work with children who have dropped out or who for a variety of reasons are unable to adjust to the demands of mainstream schools.

- Range of teaching methodologies: Within the network of alternative schools there is rich diversity of methodologies. These have emerged in response to different contexts and communities and the needs of the individual children. These different approaches have also drawn on the insights and practice of significant pioneers in education both in India and worldwide.

Global Networks of Alternative Schools

1. Montessori Schools: Montessori schools pursue an educational philosophy and methodology, characterised by a special set of didactic materials, multi age classrooms, student chosen work in longer time blocks, a collaborative environment with student mentors, absence of testing and grades, an individual and a small group instruction in academic and social skills. Many mainstream schools across the world have now adopted parts of the Montessori methodology.
2. Waldorf Schools: Also known as Steiner schools are based on the educational ideas of the philosopher Rudolf Steiner. Waldorf education is currently practised in kindergarten schools in 60 countries and is the predominant form of alternative education around the globe. Waldorf education aims at developing children and adolescents into free moral and integrated individuals through integrating practical, artistic and intellectual approaches into the teaching of all subjects.
3. Round Square Schools: Of which there are currently about 50 on all five continents and are based on concepts of experiential educational developed by Kurt Hahn, who believed that schools prepare students for life by experiencing it in an authentic learning situation as generated by work projects, community services, leadership training, international exchanges and different forms of outdoor exploration and adventure. All round square schools emphasise learning through doing with the aim of developing every student academically, physically, culturally and spiritually, through a process of self-confrontation and self-formation within the supportive environment of a school community.

4. Free or Democratic Schools: These are organised around the principles of autonomy and democracy. The oldest democratic school, Summer hill, a boarding school in southern England, was founded in 1921 by the Scottish teacher A S Neill. Sudbury Valley School, radically democratic school is situated in Massachusetts. It has served as a model for many subsequent democratic schools. Today many schools around the world describe themselves as free or democratic schools. While official rules about the organisational principles of democratic or free schools would contradict the schools' independent spirit, they share many common characteristics: decisions about the school is taken by a self-governing school body, in which each student and each teacher has one vote in a majority voting system.
5. Escuelas Nuevas: These are alternative schools started in 1987, based on the idea of improved rural and urban basic education for children from low income families. The school's pedagogy emphasises respect for the rights of children and is based on innovative educational projects involving a range of educational materials that encourage collaborative, participatory and personalised teaching methods. Schools are organised as community schools, involving the wider community as well as student's families who are invited to play an active role in school activities and their child's learning.
6. Brockwood Park School: Founded by the Indian philosopher and educator Jiddhu Krishnamurti in 1969, Brockwood Park School has a strong ethical base and focuses on both academic excellence as well as spiritual development by exploring the balance between freedom and responsibility, meditation freeing from self-centered action and inner conflict as well as appreciation and conservation of nature.
7. Dalton School: The American educational reformer Helen Parkhurst developed the Dalton laboratory Plan in 1922, which enables the students to work independently on the basis of contract, within the public-school system. Today Dalton school exists in many countries.
8. Freinet School: Freinet Schools modelled on the pedagogy of French educator Celestin Freinet, see the child's interest and natural curiosity as a starting point for learning and attempt to use real experiences of children as authentic opportunities for learning. Children are encouraged to learn cooperatively making products or providing services. In Freinet schools, students are made familiar with democratic self government to take responsibility for themselves and for their community,
9. Peter Petersen's Jenaplan School founded as a progressive education project in 1927, is based on three core ideas: autonomous students work, living and learning in a community and students and parent participation in school life. Learning takes place in mixed age groups.

A typical school day consists of a 100-minute block in which students work on an interdisciplinary project, autonomous students work on self-chosen projects as well as ritualised times of deliberation, play and celebration. Today, schools modelled on the original Jenaplan exist in Germany and Netherlands.

Two recently founded alternative schools, the Swiss Institute Beatenberg and the Canadian PROTIC serve as examples of 21st century models of alternative education, based on constructivist theories of learning.

- Institute Beatenberg focuses on the organisation of student self-efficacy and meta-cognition, thus laying a foundation for lifelong learning. Students learn alone or in small groups on self-designed learning projects coached by their teachers. They evaluate their work aided by rubrics and document learning processes and results in portfolios. Intensive training sessions and special learning days offer structured opportunities for skill development and knowledge acquisition in small group settings.
- Protic, an alternative school within a state school in Quebec City, Canada was founded in response to parent demand for modern, constructivist forms of learning. It organises the development of social, cognitive and meta-cognitive competencies through ICT supported interdisciplinary learning projects. In small groups, students solve interdisciplinary problems by means of active research, investigation and experimentation, complementary group work and the presentation of results. Self and peer evaluation using rubrics and portfolios serve to develop meta-cognitive skills as a prerequisite for lifelong learning.

Approaches of Alternative Education Programmes

Alternative education programmes range from providing opportunities for children and youth who are not enrolled in schools to design special programmes, to help children overcome the negative influences of disaster or conflict and associated trauma. Alternative education programmes are purely based on the needs and interests of the students and most of the programmes are run by governmental and non-governmental agencies. The main approaches of alternative education programmes are:

I. Alternative Access Programmes

Alternative access programmes provide an opportunity for children and youth who do not have access to education through formal schools and any other means. They provide alternative methods of delivery to fill the gap of education provision for particular age, gender or geographically isolated groups. This type of programme is developed and supported by NGOs and is essential to augment the state's provision of education or even to replace it where the capacity, resources or opportunities to provide a comprehensive education system, which are unavailable. Alternative access programme uses the formal curriculum with different pedagogical methods. There are two broad categories of Alternative access programme.

1. *Bridging Programme:*These are generally designed for children and youth who have less opportunity to go to school or who have dropped out of school. This programme enables the children to re-enter the formal school system or to complete the equivalent of the primary cycle. In India, many states organise bridges courses of different duration for mainstreaming children to formal education system. Complementary Rapid Education Programme for Schools in Sierra Leone, Alternative School Programme in Nepal and Community Oriented Primary Education Programme in Northern Uganda are the examples of bridging programme.
2. *Parallel Programmes:*These programmes are mainly for sections of the community who may be marginalised either geographically or for reasons of gender, religion, ethnicity or culture. These programmes take place in a venue other than formal school. Community schools are the example of parallel programmes.

II. Alternative Curriculum Provision

This programme is designed for the refugees and some internally displaced persons and most returnee situations and there are additional needs that develop because of the context and environment. And it is also meant for children in post natural disaster situations. Alternative curriculum provision is based on the goals of Education for All, contribution of quality education and provision of appropriate life skills for the needy students. In an emergency context, children and youth are often exposed to threatening situations that are not always directly connected to a conflict or disaster situation. Particular topics are then offered as education initiatives to respond to the needs that develop as a result of these threatening situations. Alternative curriculum can include preventive programmes as well as programmes designed to help overcome the negative consequences of conflict or disaster and associated trauma and also include life skills programmes as well as intervention strategies.

*1. Life skills programmes:*These programmes include peace and citizenship education, landmine, small arms and light weapons education, human rights education, environment education, HIV and AIDS education.

2. Psycho-social activities: The programme includes recreation, sports and cultural activities, play centres and expressive activity clubs are alternative not because of the time span of implementation but they are outside the traditional curriculum. There is a secondary reason for the alternative nature of this type of programme while the ministry may support the initiative; the impetus for the programme invariably comes from international agencies and NGOs.

III. Alternative Methodology/Pedagogy Programmes

Two alternative methodology/pedagogy programmes are being implemented in a number of countries. They are:

1. *UNICEF's Child-Friendly School Programme:* UNICEF has developed a child-friendly school programme that helps teachers to use interactive methodology and a right-based approach, which should include life skills and peace education. Through the use of interactive pedagogy, the programmes hope to build constructive attitudes and behaviours. The approach is inclusive, healthy and protective and effective for all children and involves families, communities and children too. It has a basic framework that is based on the principles of quality education. Constructive behaviour changes will occur in teacher's skill levels and attitudes. It is the aim of UNICEF to change the traditional didactic approach and so mainstream what is currently alternative.
2. *The IRC's Healing Classrooms Initiative:* The child-friendly school approach is not unique to UNICEF. The International Rescue Committee (IRC), 2005 also has a programme that attempts to mainstream content and pedagogy that are more usually considered to be alternative. Healing Classrooms is an IRC initiative implemented in more than 20 countries. It addresses teacher's role in creating supportive and healing learning environment for children. It is specifically designed to be adapted by a diverse range of people to support culturally appropriate responses and especially to suit conflict and post conflict contexts. The programmes focus on the psycho-social wellbeing of children. The training focuses on understanding the wellbeing needs of learners and associated with that, the wellbeing and motivation of teachers. The aim of the programme is to help teachers develop a safe space in the classroom and to use a right-based experiential approach to support psycho-social healing of children.

IV. Community-by-Community Approach

The community-by-community approach taken by NGOs is another form of alternative education at least in part because they work in selected communities and they do not have the right or the obligation or indeed the necessary resources to deliver a countrywide programme. The community-by-community approach obviously makes quality control easier and modifications can be made according to feedback received from the easier pilots. This approach also has the advantage of being able to choose a community that fits the profile so that the intervention is almost guaranteed to be a success. It allows a concentration of time and resources so that strong capacity can be developed before moving to the next community. This is a learner-centered approach and the ownership of the programme is firmly established.

Typology of Alternative Education

Alternative education programmes are usually defined by their characteristics, based on their focus on behaviour, interest or levels of function. Behavioural programming has to be designed by keeping in mind the needs of the students who want an organised setting in order to focus on more desirable school behaviours, which may help to facilitate their learning as well as others. Programmes are designed around the interest of the students. It might include an environmental programme or vocational academies. At the time of designing a programme, focus must be given to the educational problems or challenges that the present students are facing. Some of them are:

- During the learning stage, students are confronted with a number of problems. Students who have fallen "off track" need systems of retrieval to bring them back into high schools. The goal of getting them back into regular high schools seems to be suitable and sensible for this group.
- Students who prematurely transitioned to adulthood are forced to become parents, or have some other situations at their home which may not permit them to attend school regularly.
- Criminal track records and pregnancy may prevent the students from continuing their education. Such students who became older and 'off track' educationally because of various reasons need a smooth absorption into community colleges rapidly.
- There is a group of students who are educationally backward because of some significant problems, having very low levels of reading, over aged for grade etc. Hence, many of them have been retained repeatedly though they have come out of special education services. There exists a large populace of this kind and our present system of education lacks programmes that can cater to the needs of such groups.

Alternative educational programmes are now redesigning themselves to be smaller, innovative academic programmes for socially and academically at-risk students. These approaches are individualised and are ensured with respect for student, parent and teacher. It is all the more proved to be experiential and interest based. The students of alternative education prefer to opt for the subjects which are directly connected with their profession. It is possible to make classifications based on nature of programmes or services done by alternative education. The three level classification, known as Raywid's Typology, developed by Dr. Mary Anne Raywid, is the most discussed one. It has been described as follows.

Type I Programme

These are restructured schools offering fulltime, multilayer education options for all kinds of students, who need more individualisation, innovative or challenging curriculum, drop outs wishing to earn their diplomas etc. All these programmes offer credits, which are needed for graduation. Another characteristic of this school is divergence from standard school organisation and practices such as deregulation, flexibility, autonomy and teacher-student empowerment and special caring professional staff, small size and small classes, personalised, whole student approach that builds a sense of affiliation and features individual instruction, self-paced work and career counselling. Magnet schools, charter schools, schools without walls, experiential schools, career and job focused schools, dropout recovery programmes, after school hours and schools in a typical setting like shopping malls and museums are the examples of Type I.

Type II Programme

Discipline is the distinguishing characteristic of this type II programme, which aims to segregate, contain and reform disruptive or violent students. Students do not choose to attend but are sent to the school for specified time periods or until behaviour requirements are met. These institutions provide high school or middle school students with a mix of behaviour modification and intensive individual attention. Since placement is short term, the curriculum is limited to a few basic, required courses or is entirely supplied by the home school as a list of assignments. Familiar models include last chance schools and in-schools suspension.

Type III Programme

These are problem-solving schools. This programme provides short term but therapeutic settings for students with social and emotional problems that create academic and behavioural barriers to learning. Specially designed alternative programmes for at-risk students here tend to be non-punitive, or positive and compassionate for students in need of extra help, remediation or rehabilitation. They often provide a network of academic, social and emotional assistance to students who have been unsuccessful in the main stream.

Another important typology proposed by Melissa Roderick of the University of Chicago, puts students educational needs at front and centre rather than focusing on a student's demographic factors, risk factors and programme characteristics. This typology focuses on the educational problems or challenges present in students. Roderick identified several distinct groups.

- Students who have fallen "off track" because they have gotten into trouble and need short term systems of recovery to route them back into high schools. The goal of getting them back into regular high schools is both appropriate and realistic for this group.
- Students those who have prematurely transitioned to adulthood either because they are (about to become) parents, or have home situations that do not allow them to attend school regularly. For example immigrant children taking care of siblings while their parents work and those coming out of the juvenile justice system, etc.

- Students who have fallen substantially off track educationally, but are older and are returning to obtain the credits, need transition into community colleges very rapidly. These categories include older individuals who have just a few credits away from graduation or are transitioning out of the jail system or have had a pregnancy and are now ready to complete their secondary schooling. Roderick noted that these students are currently populating most alternative education programmes in larger urban areas; they are a very diverse group and tend to be well served by the existing alternative school system.
- The final group consists of the ones who have fallen substantially behind educationally, they have significant problems, and very low reading levels and are often over aged for grade. Many of these children have been retained repeatedly and a number of them have come out of special education. They include 17 or 18 years old with third and fourth grade reading levels who have never graduated from eighth grade. This is a very large group of youth and most of the school systems do not have any programmes that can meet their needs.

Roderick argues that by targeting a particular demographic or problem group, such as pregnant/parenting teens, programmes may be setting themselves up for failure if the students encompass too much educational diversity. As a group, pregnant/ parenting teens may include students who are two credits away from graduation, others who are wards of child welfare agencies and who have multiple problems such as being far, or over aged for grade, and yet others who have significant behavioural problems and may be weaving in and out of the juvenile justice system. No single school or programme can be expected to handle such a wide array of educational and other needs.

Strengths and Challenges of Alternative Education

The features of the effective alternative education programmes reported much strength and also reported many challenges they faced in the academic programme to help participants to succeed.

Strengths

- Small size and low teacher-student ratio: This helps to form a personal relationship between the students and teachers and individualised attention to each student's learning needs, strengths and life situations.
- Individualised academic plans: These plans are crucial for students with a range of educational issues. These plans can both map out pathways for academic success and help identify and organise a range of services and supports a student might need to achieve academic success. Some of the programmes ask students to sign a contract agreeing to this plan.
- Flexibility: Flexible scheduling of the programme is crucial for the subset of students who want or need to work or take part in a training

programme while enrolled in school. This is particularly true for students who are far behind and will need several years of academics to attain a credential.

- Academic counselling and support: This is one of the important features of the programme and often makes the difference in terms of keeping students on track, retaining them in the programme, and customising academic offerings to their needs and interests.
- Relevant curriculum: The curriculum is linked to vocational skill training and community based learning in ways that keeps students engaged and focused on the application of knowledge. There is often a career focus, guidance and opportunities for career exploration and many students in these programmes learn better through experiential learning.
- Competency based programming: Flexibility of time of the programme allows the different categories of students to master content which is more practical strategy for many students who are behind or need an accelerated curriculum because they are overage. It allows students for self-learning and self-feedback.
- Performance based assessment: Alternative education programmes allow students to demonstrate their content mastery in different ways like portfolio, project, peer assessment, journals, tests, etc.

Challenges

- Programme duration and credential attainment: Some students may not be able to attain high school diploma during the allotted time period. They need more time to achieve the goals compared with their peers. This makes lots of issues in the programme, including unrealistic targets for student and programme success and a lack of motivation of students when they are asked to reach unattainable goals.
- Creating pathways among programmes: There is a need to connect students with continuing education options that have practical steps as a large percentage of student leave programmes without credentials. Majority of the students in alternative education programmes are ready for a job or more vocational training and they need options that allow them to work while continuing school.
- Need to validate the programme: Most of the students who wish to join in alternative education programme worry that it does not always have a positive educational outcome. This has a particular concern of school districts that need to report graduation rates defined as high school diploma attainment under the rules and regulations of the country.
- Lack of effective curriculum: The materials and strategies used in teaching-learning are not suitable for all learners. It is more viable to young learners and it is more difficult for overagers. Aged learners

face so many problems handling the logical subjects like mathematics, sciences, etc.

- Lack of funds: Alternative education programmes cannot run smoothly without adequate funds. Funding structures among alternative education programmes are highly variable. Most programme budgets are based on a variety of unreliable funding sources such as grants, charitable contributions and some programmes may receive state and local education funds, although these funds are often less than the per pupil funding those formal schools receives.
- Lack of connection among higher education programme: Many of the programmes have a few opportunities for the higher education of the learners.
- Difficulty for getting teachers: Teacher's pay and benefits are often lower than formal school, so there is a difficulty in attracting and retaining qualified teachers.
- Need for strategies for multilevel classroom: Most alternative education learners are of different academic levels and have different needs with different age groups. So, need for strategies to differentiate instructions for different levels of learners in the same classroom rather than have all students to work individually all the time.
- Administrative problem: The success of the alternative education programme depends on its administration. Programmes are sponsored or administered by a variety of agencies or organisations. There is no specific literature that relates specifically to administrative accountability. So, this creates problem.

Studies examine the effectiveness of alternative education programmes in terms of student outcomes. Work has advanced on what types of outcome measures should be targeted and monitored. Alternative education programmes are first and foremost educational programmes, so they need to focus on preparing students academically while also meeting the individual needs of their students. There is a question on how to introduce high academic standards in alternative education system without sacrificing the elements that make alternative programmes successful and without compromising the integrity of the high standards. Recommendations designed to strengthen the adoption of high standards by alternative education programme includes:

- Improving early warning systems to identify lower performing students;
- Collecting and analysing student level data;
- Developing enhanced general education diploma programmes;
- Developing data-driven accountability measures for alternative education programmes;
- Strengthening links between traditional and non-traditional education systems;

- Investing resources to support the transition to high academic standards and beyond; and
- Supporting long term alternative education programmes.

Characteristics of High-quality Alternative Education Programmes

Researchers and policy makers are even now assessing the qualities of a promising alternative educational programme. Unfortunately records of all those qualities are starting to converge and point to the variables that should be gauged and supervised. Therefore, more laborious assessments are to be conducted. These characteristics are thought to be indispensable for the accomplishment of efforts taken for imparting alternative education and are described as follows.

High Academic Standards: Alternative education is designed in such a way to ensure maximum attainment of high academic standards. Hence, successful programmes/schools possess well defined higher standards of education and prospects for their children. The curriculum in this programme is very powerful as there is no kind of dilution or watering down done anywhere. Furthermore, the curricula also ensure the development of the educational and vocational interests of the students.

Academic Instruction: All successful programmes have a clear focus on the academic learning based on high academic standards along with some well engaged and highly creative instructional methods. They also have high expectations from all students. It must be ensured that the learning happening in such programmes has to be much relevant and must be applicable to the big life outside school. It also must ensure future work opportunities for students. Such programmes have academically rigorous curricula. They are also tied to state standards and accountability systems.

Here, the students, staff and parents know and share their goals of learning. All the students in such a system have personalised learning plans too. They set individual learning goals based on their particular plans. In this system, there are openings for the youth to catch up and accelerate their knowledge and skills too. A variety of instructional approaches is also available to help them to achieve their academic objectives.

Instructional Staff: The instructors who are involved in successful alternative programmes use positive discipline techniques and always establish good rapport with their students and peers. They keep high expectations about the youth and their students. They are very creative in their classrooms too. They play big roles in governing the school and also in designing the programmes and curriculum.

Professional Development: The biggest source of information for the students has always been the teachers. As such, teachers have the responsibility to be very talented and they should also be ready to update themselves with the latest. By understanding this very well, many good and successful schools around us provide teachers with ongoing professional development training and activities that stimulate and help them to maintain an academic focus thereby enhancing their teaching strategies and new alternative instructional methods. Such properly designed staff development activities involve teacher input, work with colleagues and opportunities to visit and observe teaching in other settings. When they are given such opportunities to scrutinise differences between instructional aspirations and actual practice, teachers will surely achieve what they aspire to do. So, it is always recommendable to have such well designed and well defined staff development programmes.

Size: It is necessary to remember the fact that every student in the class needs to be properly attended to develop his/her skills. Therefore, if the number of students in a class is on the higher side, the quality and time span of individual attention from the teachers will be less. Small teacher-student ratio is essential for the success of any efforts in alternative education. Successful efforts, it is observed, have an average teacher-student ratio of 1:16.

Social Interactions/Interpersonal skills: It is undoubtedly clear that education plays a significant role in helping people develop their interactive skills. Successful alternative education programmes/schools are equipped with well defined standards of behaviours with precise and accurate expectations that are consistently applicable to everyone. Also, they possess the curricula that are expanded in such a way to foster the maximum development of interpersonal and social skills. They also address issues related with family life, peer pressure and conflict resolution etc.

Student Centred Education and Intervention Plans: The most important aim of alternative educational programme is the development of the capabilities of students. Successful programmes/schools design their structure, curricula and support services in such a way that it addresses both the educational and social needs of the students. They are packed with many assessment and support services which are needed for a clear identification and address issues related with cognitive, emotional health and also the socio-economic factors which are likely to affect the education and development of participating students.

Leadership, Governance and Administration: Alternative education programmes highlight the importance of having an administrative and bureaucratic autonomy. They also need to be devoid of any rigidity and must contain much operational flexibility. All concerned and connected with the movement like administrators, teachers, support services staff, students and parents should be very much involved in the various aspects of the programme. The autonomy provided will build trust and loyalty among the staff. A good and successful alternative education programme must have a strong and committed leadership which is very much involved and engaged in it. It is preferable if the leadership is entrusted with a teacher/director administering the programme.

Parent and Community Involvement: Parents and community surely have a significant role to ensure the continuation of the education of the school dropouts. Their involvement plays a decisive role in the success of alternative programmes/schools. It is indicated by the fact that all the programmes and schools that came in various related research projects found that the involvement of the parents in clearly defined ways beyond parent-teacher meetings were important in its success. Some needed parents to spend some of their time to the programme/school. Some others needed their participation in various seminars.

Mostly such schools give attention on the creation and maintenance of communities. Such intentional communities made with good purposes are more likely to succeed well than their bureaucratically ruled counterparts. In some of such school communities, students and staff share common expectations for learning. There, students are continuously encouraged to take a variety of courses and activities that will enable them to pursue their interests and ambitions.

Programme vs School: The alternative education must be based on either programmes or schools. Programmes are meant for students who need short term interventions in order to survive a specific problem or situation which may have a negative impact on their education. They are designs made with the goal of assisting the students to retrieve into the regular school setting as soon as the present problem or situation is attended and amended.

But on the other hand, schools are designed for students who for one or the other reason will be better off by acquiring an education outside the conventional school ambience. Very often, these types of schools include students who must work to help and support themselves and their families or sometimes they are students who need specialised services and interventions and can meet high standards and achievements in education.

Locality: One important factor that determines the success of alternative education programmes or school is its locality. In fact, programmes are often set within a traditional school itself. Sometimes they are located within a community school or agency. On the other hand, a majority of the alternative schools either have their own facilities or share a facility with a larger school or are located within community colleges or a university campus. Irrespective of the location, successful programmes and schools afford advantageous physical environments that promote education, emotional wellbeing and also a sense of pride and safety.

Focus on Academic Learning: A clear focus is also very much essential for the effective implementation of an alternative education programme. Most of the promising schools in this segment have a clear focus on academic learning. They combine high academic standards with engaging and creative instructions.

Decision-making: Decision-making is a major player in determining the success of alternative education programmes. Delivering effective services requires decision-making at the level of service delivery. Various decisions related to budgeting, staffing, curriculum, leadership, scheduling and pedagogy need to be made by teaching and supporting staff. Successful schools do not hesitate to provide autonomy as far as it is possible. This certainly helps to build trust and loyalty among the staff. Giving the staff such a role and voice in decision making also promotes creativity as well as instructional excellence.

One very interesting angle or aspect of this list is how appealing and universal it is. Of course, it will also certainly appear that these are also the qualities that would seem to benefit any educational programme and not just the alternative ones. This clearly supports another idea too. The current approaches to alternative education may be defined by and are understood as being different from mainstream educational options. However, there is a vision for future that all communities have a lot of high quality educational options that will result in sharing many of these desirable characteristics.

2

Agencies of Alternative Education

Governmental Agencies

The powerlessness of the formal education systems to make education available to everyone with the existing structures and system paved the way for the development of novel structures of education. These structures are usually categorised under alternative systems of education. Initiatives put forward by Central and State governments for alternative education are increasing day by day in the form of schemes meant for non-formal education like formation of national and state level open schools, alternative schools at the elementary, secondary and tertiary levels of education etc. The Government of India's Education Guarantee Scheme and Alternative and Innovative Education scheme under the Sarva Shiksha Abhiyan employ flexible strategies for out of school children, including bridge course, back to school camps and residential camp for accelerated learning.

Education Guarantee Scheme (EGS)

Madhya Pradesh Government started this initiative in 1997. The aim of this programme was to provide educational opportunities for weaker sections living in extreme remote areas. This scheme was based upon the principles of decentralisation and community participation. So, the EGS teacher, known as Guruji was appointed by Janapad Panchayat Shiksha Samiti. Through this scheme, academic inputs, availability of teacher with basic educational qualifications and community involvement in school management increases sense of local ownership in education system. Now, EGS is a part of Sarva Shiksha Abhiyan and it promotes decision-making on the part of the community with regard to their educational requirements.

Alternative Schooling Programme (ASP)

This programme was conceptualised by Rajiv Gandhi Prathamik Shiksha Mission in 1994-95. ASP was perceived not just as the non-formal option to the formal system but in fact, as an effort to create an effective teaching-learning flexible process so as to respond with sensitivity to learners' needs moving beyond the structurally dichotomised categories of formal and non-formal streams. No concept of pass or fail in ASP and students can be different levels in different subjects. ASP is thought of as an alternative system of education for the children of 6-14 years of age who are unable to participate in formal schooling for a variety of reasons like, being engaged in household activities, helping parents for supplementing family income, living in extreme remote areas and migrating to other places for work. The working hours, timing and appointment of the teachers in ASP was decided by the District Panchayat on the recommendations of Village Panchayat or School Management Committee. Teachers have to be local persons with a minimum qualification of X class pass and 21 days of intensive training for teachers before joining the ASP. This programme attempted to introduce an intermediate or bridge model for increasing access to 'out of school' children.

Lok Jumbish Project (LJP)

Rajasthan Government launched this programme in 1992 with an aim of achieving universal elementary education in remote backward villages with participation of communities. This programme addresses the needs of the children who have been left out of the mainstream educational system and also catered to the education of children from minority communities and children with disabilities.

Shiksha Karmi Project (SKP)

Shiksha Karmi Project was started in Rajasthan in 1987 with an aim of qualitative improvement in remote and socially backward villages with a primary focus on gender. The project was launched to remove the major obstacles in achieving universal elementary education, namely, teacher absenteeism, high dropout rate, working children, uninteresting teaching methods, lack of contextual learning materials, low motivation and competence of teachers, a centralised and inflexible approach etc. with a special emphasis on community participation. The innovative crux of the project was the substitution of primary school teachers by a team of two locally recruited resident educational workers called Shiksha Karmis. Village Education Committees were involved to improve the school environment augmentation and infrastructure facilities, for a larger enrolment of children through school mapping and micro-planning in the Shiksha Karmi schools.

Mahila Samakhya

Mahila Samkhya was started in 1989 with external assistance focusing on gender. It aimed at promoting education and empowerment of rural women, particularly women in socially and economically marginalised groups and helping them to overcome social barriers and address issues such as child marriage, child labour, violence against women, etc. Women collectives established under this programme have established centres for educating girls who have dropped out of the system and adolescent and working girls.

Janshala Programme

The Janshala programme was launched in 1988. It was a collaborative effort of Government of India and five UN agencies and they provided programme support to the ongoing efforts towards achieving UEE. The agencies are UN Development Programme (UNDP), UNICEF, UNESCO, International Labour Organisation (ILO) and UNFPA Janshala was a community based primary education programme that aimed at making primary education more accessible and effective, especially for girls and children in deprived communities, marginalised groups, SC/STs, minorities, working children and children with special needs. Janshala started a large number of alternative schools in small and remote habitations in the programme areas, besides evolving strategies and setting up schools with community participation in the urban slums. The major areas of achievement are teacher training, multi grade teaching, intervention for education of the disabled, setting up of block and cluster resource centres and strengthening capacities at the state, district and block levels.

National Programme on Education of Girls at Elementary Level (NPEGEL)

NPEGEL has been formulated for education of under-privileged/disadvantaged girls from Class I to VIII as a separate and district gender component plan of SSA. The main objective of NPEGEL is to develop and promote facilities to provide access and to facilitate retention of girls and to ensure greater participation of women and girls in the field of education. The NPEGEL includes the education of out of school girls, over age girls, who have not completed elementary education, working girls, and girls from marginalised social groups, girls with low attendance due to their problems and girls with low level of achievement.

Kasturba Gandhi Balika Vidyalaya (KGBV)

The Government of India approved KGBV with the existing schemes of Sarva Shiksha Abhiyan. The objective of KGBV is to ensure access and quality education to the girls of the disadvantaged groups of society by setting up residential schools with boarding facilities at the elementary level. KGBV tackling gender specific issues that prevent girls and women from having access to education, providing women and adolescent girls with necessary support structure, and an informal learning environment to create opportunities for education and helping girls to overcome socio-cultural and economic factors inhibiting their access to elementary education.

Non-governmental Agencies

Many non-governmental organisations also made some good work in the field of alternative education. They offer chances to the disadvantaged, school dropouts and street children for having basic education by implementing new methods thereby improving the quality of education. This leads to an alternative schooling experience. Voluntary contribution in the field of education has incessantly played an important role in accomplishing the requirements of disadvantaged children. In particular, substitutive means for education are offered to girls and it played a major role in education through duplication of their models and through policy dialogue with the government. Voluntarism comes out as an ideology and was connected with the liberalisation and was projected as a good alternative.

In India, the number of registered NGOs increased immensely during the last two decades. NGOs have played enormous and different roles with their own work, through association with the state, its agencies and community. Various projects introduced by the government of diverse states as well as centrally sponsored schemes for refining the education, health and development sectors have witnessed massive contributions of NGOs in accomplishing the targeted goals. Their partaking has been found as an effective alternative to put into effect the programmes without mediators, bureaucratic tangles and formalities. There are many NGOs working in the field of education, predominantly at the primary education level in the states and local level.

MV Foundation (MVF)

It is a private charitable trust providing educational opportunities for working children into the ambit of school education. The foundation takes up community issues related to education. The foundation gives awareness and motivates parents and children to use formal school as a medium for advancement. They arranged different strategies for working children, bridge courses in summer camps and long duration camps for those who are in the age group of secondary level.

Pratham Council for Vulnerable Children (PCVC)

Pratham is a non-governmental agency started in 1994 with UNICEF support, to provide quality education to the underprivileged children. Pratham set up by PCVC in 2001 which has been working with vulnerable and working children to help them to receive basic education and lead them to a better life. The other programmes of the council are prevention, rehabilitation, repatriation, rescue and education of vulnerable and working children. The PCVC built up a number of residential schools to teach children who have been rescued but no chances to return to their home.

Bodh Shiksha Samiti (BSS)

BSS was launched in Rajasthan in 1987 with an objective to provide education of socially marginalised groups. They give a strong orientation to slum children towards equity in provisions and opportunities. Participation of motivated youth in schooling of slum children was the mainstay of the initiative. The samiti itself trained the identified people intensively.

Nirantar

Nirantar, a resource centre for gender and education was started in 1993. It works towards enabling empowering education, especially for girls and women from marginalised communities. Nirantar has done its activities through direct field interventions, training and capacity building, creating educational resources and research and advocacy. Nirantar is actively involved with women's movement and other democratic rights movements and brings concerns central to those movements into their educational work.

Agragamee

Agragamee's primary education programme seeks to develop a model of qualitative education for tribal children who are unable to access primary education for a variety of reasons. The schools have had a significant interaction with other schools in the locality, to give a wide exposure to the children. Agragamee also instituted to promote aspects of tribal development and to adopt an integrated approach to help tribal communities mobilise for self-sustainability. They look to build an institutional base for training tribal youth as well as young educated professionals

Katha

Katha is a Delhi-based NGO founded by Geeta Dharmarajan in 1989. It works in the field of community development, child welfare, education and literature. The organisation works for achieving social justice and curbing poverty in urban India and it connects the basic work in education, urban resurgence and story. Katha is working for the welfare of the children in slums and it runs a non-conventional school, KITES (Katha Information Technology and E-commerce School) in slum area of Delhi. The mission of this organisation lies in enabling every child to live in productive life through quality education and enhanced reading skills that unleashes individual potential and creates opportunities.

Individual and Corporate Agencies

The alternative education movement believes that each child is distinctive, so special attention needs to be given to each child. The child must be addressed in wholeness and not in shattered parts. It becomes the highest responsibility of the education system to bring up fantasy as well as imagination in a child. When children grow to become adolescents then they must be encouraged to develop independent thinking along with idealism. This kind of educational system will guarantee that when they grow into adults, they will have new ways and visions not only for themselves, but for the entire human race. Indian subcontinent, during the twentieth century, reveals that the larger part of initiatives were there, either acts of private philanthropy or instituted by freedom fighters, social activists etc. The schools established included formal schools and those based on alternative philosophies of education and work. After independence, some of the alternative initiatives lost their lustre due to spreading of the formal system, a few flourished and some were revived later and managed by trusts or non-governmental agencies. These initiatives were specifically rooted in different philosophies and were started not only by educational reformers, freedom fighters and philosophers but also more recently by industrialists and multinational corporates. As the importance of alternative education initiatives continues to grow stronger due to the highly diverse nature of the society today, the private philanthropic contribution by individuals, organisations and non-governmental agencies have contributed significantly in developing and sustaining alternative education programmes.

Corporate Social Responsibility (CSR) programmes have done a significant contribution in Indian development. CSR takes a number of citizenship activities. Most of these organisations accomplish their activities close to home by rendering services for encouraging people who live in villages, towns and districts near where the organisations function. CSR is not a novel idea in India; companies like Tata and Birla have been the case of social goodness and private philanthropy in education such as opening schools and colleges for better education. These companies began their operations decades before CSR became a well-liked cause. In spite of having such life size successful examples, CSR in India is still in a variety nascent stage. A lot of needs are to be accomplished in the India's development sector. Now, CSR in India has gone beyond merely charity and donations. It has become a vital part of the corporate strategy. CSR programmes could range from the general development of a community to supporting specific causes like education, environment, health care, etc.

NaiTalim or Basic Education

This initiative was conceived by Mahatma Gandhi based on his vision of a good society. NaiTalim aimed to flourish education and give freedom from ignorance, literacy superstition psyche of servitude and many other taboos that inhibited in free thinking of independent India. According to Gandhiji's words and vision, NaiTalim was aimed at becoming the spearhead of a silent social revolution. NaiTalim was the preparation and practice for the peaceful organisation of a cooperative human community and non-violence finds a place in the education. The major idea of NaiTalim is the provision of basic or primary education in child-centric and inter-related manner to enrich the character of the child.

However, the NaiTalim is now rejuvenated by the NaiTalim Samiti, thereby taking up the initiative and the responsibility to restart the school at Sevagram. Thus, Anand Niketan was reopened at Sevagram in July, 2005. Its basic principles are based on Gandhiji's ideas on education and are considered to be appropriate today though they emerged 75 years ago. The Anand Niketan NaiTalim school at Sevagram together with Teacher's Training Institute at various levels of learning activities from pre-primary to rural university is an exceptional and path breaking experiment. It takes into consideration the developments of educational thoughts and the challenges in modern context.

Indian Institute of Education (IIE)

J.P. Naik and R.V. Parulekar founded IIE in 1948 in Bombay with an aim of making social justice and equality in independent India through education.

In 1976, IIE was shifted to Pune for better facilities and scope for outreach programmes, projects and other related activities. IIE believes that properly planned and organised education can serve as an effective stimulus for evolving an egalitarian society based on the principle of social justice, freedom and dignity of the individual. The institute gives more importance to the development of non-formal education than intervening in the formal system and trying out measures for converting the formal education system based on the needs of the disadvantaged sections of the society. The IIE model of community managed basic education is recognised by the Ministry of Human Resources and Development and used this model with local modifications which can be fitted into its flexible character. District Primary Education Programme of State Education Department adopted some of the features of IIE model.

Grambal Shiksha Kendra

Anutai Wagh, an educationist worked for tribal children and developed an alternative approach for their education. The education starts with basic cleanliness and hygiene with indigenous material support using locally available materials from the flora and fauna of the region, pebbles, seeds, leaves, fruits and mud become the means to arithmetic and clay work. She designed vocational courses which would enable them to earn while they learn. This helps them to set up technical trades like carpentry, tailoring, pottery and other cottage industries.

Gram Mangal

In 1982, Anutai established another venture, Gram Mangal as a registered non-government organisation working in the field of tribal education. The working area of GM is pre-primary and primary education. They conduct one-year training programme for tribal children. The main feature of the GM work is tailor-made education programme for tribal children. GM started a form of school, Vikaswadi, a multi-level non-graded school, which takes into account the problems of tribal children who are the first-generation learners. Tribal habitats are scattered and there are about 35 to 40 children in each Vikaswadi. The innovative approach of GM has received appreciation from both the government and the NGOs working in the field of education.

Friends of Tribal Society (FTS) or Vanbandhu Parishad

FTS is one of the organisations under the Ekal Abhiyan, the largest NGO in India. FTS is an alternative school established in 1989 for educating tribal people/children with the main objective of improving literacy and health. The schools run a four prolonged programmes like, primary education, health care education, development education and empowerment education to make the tribals healthy, strong and gainfully employed. The model of basic education adopted by FTS is low cost, indigenous and covers more the teaching of numbers and alphabets. This model, not only imparts comprehensive education, but also develops values and culture in children.

Adharshila Learning Centre

Adharshila is one of the leading alternative education programmes in the country established in 1998. It is more than a place for learning, it is a children's space, an experiment in education and a stepping stone. The main objective of Adharshila Learning Centre is exploring new possibilities in the field of tribal education. It is a place to do experimented ideas in education. Holistic approach to learning is the important feature of this centre. Here students are divided into different groups based on their age and ability and provide opportunity for regular discussions and critical thinking exercises to create awareness about their society and their identity. Learning process is structured in an interdisciplinary way, providing materials to students and encourages learning themselves. This makes the children more serious about their studies and other works. The centre gives some responsibilities to students to handle some works like, cleaning, maintain library, handle electrical problems, run small shops and banks, handle small health problems, etc. A wholesome learning experience is provided to children by adopting a flexible curriculum in which there is a sufficient scope to include academics, world issues, practical skills and cultural heritage. It is totally a fun-filled learning experience for children.

Salaam Balak Trust (SBT)

Mira Nair, the director of the movie *Salaam Bombay*, was the real inspiration behind the starting of Salaam Balak Trust in Mumbai in 1989. The movie *Salaam Bombay* was released in 1988 and the main actors of this movie are the real street children in Mumbai. Before starting the movie, she conducted an acting workshop and the response of these children was really amazing. The crew of the movie was inspired by the response of these children and they understood that these children need necessary assistance for making a move from the street to mainstream life. The trust helped thousands of children for a safe and nurturing environment in its function in the past years and they provided a holistic safety services catering to the individual needs of Mumbai street children. SBT gives services to the entire areas of child development from physical, medical, educational, social and vocational needs of the children.

Tamana

Tamana, a non-profit voluntary organisation was registered in 1984, in the name of Shyma Chona's daughter Tamana Chona, who was born with cerebral palsy. At Tamana, individual educational programmes are formed for every child, integrating elements of special education, regular academic programme through the NIOS, therapeutic interventions and vocational training. The aim of such programmes is to build up socially and economically autonomous children.

The provisions offered at each centre of Tamana embrace speech occupational and physiotherapy, life skill training, computer education, music and dance, weight management and physical fitness, sports and extracurricular activities, counselling, behaviour modification, diagnosis and assessment facilities and family counselling. All-inclusive development of each child with the help of a personalised education plan for each child is the main objective of this organisation. The personalised education plan comprises of numerous areas of development, including development of language, communication, fine motor skills and interpersonal social skills. The potency of their programmes lies in their emphasis on the child's strengths and interest, thereby making education more functional and age appropriate as possible.

Amar Jyoti Research and Rehabilitation Centre

Amar Jyoti Research and Rehabilitation Centre is one of the most important organisations started for children with disability in 1981 at Delhi. It was under the control of Amar Jyoti Charitable Trust. It extends rehabilitative services to persons with disabilities. This was done through an integrated approach of inclusive education, medical care, vocational training, child guidance and self-employment. In classrooms, children learn together from nursery to Class VIII. Children with problems of development delays like hearing and visual impairments and those with multiple disabilities are kept in separate sections. Equal opportunities are given to them in all other activities like sports, cultural programmes, vocational training, etc. The school also has provisions for language, computer and science labs. It was set with the objective of having inclusivity and providing comprehensive services, under the guidance of professionals in each area.

Shiv Nadar Foundation

Sri Shiv Nadar, an industrialist and philanthropist and the founder and chairman of HCL had taken an alternative education initiative in mid-1990. His efforts are focussed towards the educational development of India. For that he started many educational institutions and one among them, Vidya Gyan schools, is a radical social experiment in nurturing leadership from amongst highly gifted rural poor children. These schools are social enterprise that aim to induct and transform meritorious rural children from economically disadvantaged backgrounds, by providing them free world class education. The foundation is setting up world class schools aiming to provide children with an education for life.

Azim Premji Foundation

It is a non-profit organisation that has been working since 2000 with the elementary education system in India in rural government schools. They began by implementing various programmes to improve educational quality across the country. Foundation has run schools for the children of migrant labour and worked with community and collaborated with different educational programmes in curriculum, pedagogy, assessment, teacher education and school management.

Citi Group

Citi group, a corporate one, supports education of the underprivileged in the country. They believe that economic development of the country is accelerated through the education of the children of that country. They provide primary education facilities to underprivileged children. Citi group identified economically underprivileged communities and slum pockets and give them educational needs.

Michael and Susan Dell Foundation (MSDF)

This is established in 1999 with an aim to create opportunities to direct and measurably transform the lives of children living in urban poverty. The programmes of MSDF focussed in five areas: Child health, Education, Safety, Youth development and Early Childhood Care.

Tech Mahindra Foundation

Tech Mahindra foundation was launched in 2007. This foundation is meant to address the educational empowerment of the underprivileged children and women. The programmes of the foundation are in alignment with its vision of bringing about sustainable changes, aimed at economically less privileged and socially disadvantaged.

Chirag Foundation

Chirag foundation started in 2005 with activities for children providing them with fundamental education to develop into competent and confident individuals. The aim is to make a difference in the lives of children who are deprived of opportunities and equip them to face the competitive world with pride and good character.

3

Indian Educational Thinkers on Alternative Education

Indian education system has witnessed a number of structural or paradigm shifts over the concept of alternative education. Non-formal education in the Indian context has developed a narrow meaning of an alternative delivery system of education for children who are not able to join the formal elementary school due to one or the other reasons. In this context, the non-formal education has been limited to provision of a second chance or alternative opportunities for out of school children to complete their basic education. Non-formal education as an alternative to formal education was experienced with as early as 1976 in the country. About this time, efforts were made to come out with the definitions or meanings of various terms used synonymously and interchangeably under the umbrella term alternative education. Many educationist and philosophers express their ideas about the education which is useful for every community member. Many of them were against the British education system, which is followed before and after independence. Some of them express their ideas and experiments in educational system about the alternative form of education. Here we discuss about those thinkers.

Mahatma Gandhi

Gandhiji conceived his basic education programme as against colonial British education which is impractical and destructive of Indian tradition, imagination and culture. He expressed his ideas and activities through Sabarmati and Sevagram ashrams. The school inmates worked, prayed and ate together. Gandhi's scheme of national education with its emphasis on craft as the axis of education came to be known as Basic Education, Buniyadi Shiksha and NaiTalim.

According to Gandhi, education is not a "Pouring in Process" but a "drawing out Process". The focus of knowledge does not lie "outside" but "within" the child. Gandhi says, by education I mean an all-round drawing out of the best in child and man – body, mind and spirit. This concept of education draws attention to two things: education is a drawing out process and that the drawing out should be all round and comprehensive aiming at the three dimensions of human personality i.e., body, mind and spirit.

Individual lost his/her freedom due to economic, social and political subjugation and he believed that through education, liberation of the individual and nation would happen. Based on this, he formulated the aims of education.

Aims of Education

Aims of education as Gandhi said are:

Self-sufficiency aim: For fulfilling this aim, he started craft centred basic education system. This makes the individual economically independent and self-sufficient and it works as insurance agent of unemployment.

Cultural aim: Gandhiji said, British education aimed cultural conquest and individual alienation and their curriculum dissociated the individuals from the socio-cultural milieu. He emphasised that preservation and transmission of Indian culture and ideal citizenship training are the main aims of education.

Character building aim: The aim of education is not to fill the mind of the child with knowledge, it is to build its character so he believed individual is essentially moral in nature. So, education is to raise man to a higher moral and spiritual order through full development of his personality.

For fulfilling these aims of education, Gandhiji started basic education with the basic principle of non-violence. Implementing free and compulsory education and craft centred education, he aimed at attaining self-sufficiency. Gandhiji believed that foreign language is responsible for cultural conquest so he adopts vernacular as medium of education. Child and activity centred methods are adopted for teaching-learning. He made an attempt to correlate school knowledge with life. This attempts to establish an interrelationship between various subjects and subject knowledge with real life. In Gandhian scheme, teacher-pupil relationship is not established through syllabus or curriculum, but through both adopting same pattern of life. Their relationship is a living relationship.

According to Gandhiji, teaching methods should be child centred and activity centred. He wanted to implement a mode of education where learning and doing are fused together. It makes teaching a joyful activity. Gandhian method looks pragmatic and naturalistic and the aim was to make man one with nature. Gandhiji's method gives a strong ethical base to his education. Gandhiji treated knowledge as a compact whole and tried to establish a reciprocal relationship between various subjects of the curriculum. These help for a better understanding of the curriculum and also correlate school knowledge with life. This helps to bind education to the child's life and beyond.

Rabindranath Tagore

According to Tagore, education should be in full touch with our complete life—economic, cultural, aesthetic, social, spiritual and educational. So educational philosophy of Tagore centred on the autonomy of the child, creative self-expression, active communication with nature and human beings and liberationist pedagogy.

Autonomy of the child: Tagore followed the naturalist philosophy of Rousseau which believes in the freedom of the child. He was against the oppressive schooling that negated the freedom of the child and he advocated that childhood was a time of freedom from specialisation, social and professional conventionalism.

Creative self-expression: It is the integral part of his educational philosophy. He, both as an individualist and a naturalist, believes that every child in the process of natural development seeks its self-expression. He thinks that creative expression takes varied forms like music, dance, sculpture, painting, poetry and labour.

Active communication with nature and humans: Creative expression is possible only when the child freely communes with nature and humans. Commune with nature is not sufficient for the child to express itself and to have active commune with humans and society.

Liberationist Pedagogy: Tagore wanted to liberate children from oppressive practices inflicted on them in the name of civilisation.

Tagore was against the existing concept of school, "Schools became education factories, lifeless, colourless and disassociated from the context of the universe, within the bare white walls staring like eyeballs of the dead." His conception about school was as a natural, open, free and communal educational environment which would arouse imagination, emotions, and knowledge. School would be located in nature and at the same time communal in organisation, no desk, bench or classrooms. Children would be free to organise their own immediate environment. In the late 1890s Tagore started a school, Sealdah, the headquarters of his estate, teaching various subjects including English. Englishman would teach children English. The Ashram school at Shanti Niketan was founded in 1901 on the basis of the ancient Indian forest schools. In 1909, he started another school Tapovan — forest school was typical of the Indian system of education with its emphasis on the basic elements of Indian culture. Later, Tagore updated this form of school to include science and similar modern subjects and the Shanti Niketan School developed continuously, the school called Patha Bhawan. Later he established a school for rural reconstruction work called Shikshasastra and Sree Niketan with the objectives to provide an all-round education for village children, enabling them to earn a decent livelihood, but also equipping them to improve rural life in all its aspects.

Tagore emphasised cultural subjects in the construction of curriculum and gave importance to co-curricular activities. He criticised static education within the classroom, that divorce between the body and mind without integration.

Also, he criticised bookish knowledge and examination-oriented teaching and advocated constructive and creative activities. He stressed the movement of whole body in various learning activities. Teaching while walking is the best method of teaching. According to Tagore, central point in educational activity is Joy and he emphasised the principle of curiosity, interest and spirit of play. Method of learning is to bring the child's mind in contact with nature. Tagore believed in self-learning of the child and enunciated three principles in a child's self-education: freedom, fullness and vastness. He advocated fullness of experience — physical, mental, aesthetic and emotional. Tagore also mentioned the importance of the teacher and the main function of the teacher is to produce an atmosphere for creative activity.

Vivekananda

Vivekananda looks at education from the Vedanta perspective, i.e., Spiritual nature of ultimate reality, essential divinity of man and innateness of knowledge. According to him, education is the manifestation of perfection that is already in man. His concept of education is a blend of Vedantic spiritual knowledge and science based western secular knowledge with an inherent bias towards spirituality. He visualised a system of education that would attack social evils like superstition, poverty, illiteracy etc. He wanted education to be nationalistic, "We must have the whole education of our country, spiritual and secular, in our hands, and it must be on national lines and through national methods as far as practicable." He wanted people to have an education that would enable them to stand up, functioning as free individual, proud of their past, sure of their future, with integrated personalities and devoting themselves to work for their own upliftment and the service of the nation. Vivekananda advocated universal education; its theoretical base was the equality of all human beings. He says, if poor cannot come to school for education, education should go to them. He was very interested to see that women got opportunities to get educated.

Vivekananda was against the education that was concentrating on the development of the intelligence. He wanted to awake the youth not only from spiritual ignorance but also from social and political ignorance. So, according to him, the ultimate aim of education is spiritual self-realisation and salvation. But he did not lose sight of immediate material, social and political self. He wanted to have an educational programme that would arouse the social consciousness among the youth. This will help to create an awareness of understanding among fellow beings and their living conditions. Vivekananda suggested that social service should be the criteria for selecting students for higher education.

Vivekananda constituted a curriculum within the framework of vedantic spiritual understanding including yoga, vedantic scriptures, science and technology, vocational and technical education, history and English. He says, essence of education is concentration of mind and not the collection of facts. So, the learner has to become active and attentive and concentration is the method of learning. He warned against uncritical acceptance of any form of knowledge whatever its source and everyone has a capacity to judge knowledge based on one's own experience. So, we use reason as a method of learning and also he advocated the use of audio-visual aids in teaching. Vivekananda had the modern idea about the teacher, the teacher can help, but the student has to draw on himself. The external teacher offers only the suggestion, which arouses the internal teacher to work to understand things.

Aurobindo

Aurobindo propounded the philosophy of integral education. He criticised the contemporary educational system, which completely ignores the child psychology and laboriously loading the child's mind with outdated knowledge in the name of education. Imparting information is not education; education should begin with and built on sound theoretical understanding of the child. The chief aim of education should be to help the growing soul to draw out that itself which is best and make it perfect for a noble use. So, the duty of the educationist is to develop in the child the right use of the six senses. Not only that the utilisation of the super mind for the development of an integrated human personality should be the true aim of education.

For achieving the integration of mind with super mind, integration of all the dimensions of human personality is necessary. So, the individual must have five principal aspects corresponding to the five principal activities of the human being. The activities are physical, vital, mental, psychic and spiritual. Educational activities intended to develop the five principal aspects of integrated human personality constitute the curriculum of integral education.

Physical education: The education of the body should begin at birth and continue throughout life. Physical education has three principal aspects — control and discipline of the functioning of the body, integral, methodological and harmonious development of all parts and movements of the body, and correction of the defects and deformities.

Vital education: This is the education of the senses and this is based on two principal aspects — development and use of sense organs and progressing awareness and control of the character — culminating in its transformation. Education of the senses will have very happy effects even on character, which is the second component of the vital education.

Mental education: The mental education will prepare man for a higher life through five principle phases:

1. development of the power of concentration, the capacity of attention;
2. development of the capacities of expansion, widening, complexity and richness;
3. organisation of one's idea around a central idea, a higher ideal or a supremely luminous idea that will serve as a guide in life;

4. thought control, rejection of undesirable thought to become able to think only what one wants and when one wants;
5. development of mental silence, perfect calm and a more and more total receptivity to inspiration coming from the higher regions of the being.

Mental education assumes all comprehensive treatment in integral education.

Psychic and spiritual education: Psychic education takes care of the internal being of the individual and it aims at high realisation upon earth. Spiritual education is an escape from all earthly manifestation, even from the whole universe, a return to the un-manifest. Psychic and spiritual education intended for preparing the mind for judging the spiritual things and hence it needs supra mental education.

Aurobindo expressed his views about teaching.

1. Nothing can be taught: Nothing can be imposed upon the mind of the child from outside since the mind evolves from within.
2. The child should be consulted in his growth: While providing education, one must take into account needs as well as the will of the individual child.
3. The child should be led from near to far or known to unknown.

According to Aurobindo, teaching job is not transmitting knowledge to the child, but only to help and guide the child in his pursuit of knowledge. Sri Aurobindo's philosophy is practised in Auro schools managed by Sri. Aurobindo Foundation for Integral Education and Research (SAFIER) and Indian Council for Integral Education (ICIE), Mirambika Free Profress School at New Delhi and other organisations run by the society.

Jiddu Krishnamurthy

Jiddu Krishnamurthy is a critic of present education system, especially the educational aims, content and physicality of educational centres. He comments on the theory-leadenness of education, excessive and exclusive emphasis on technique and neglect of the human dimension. The over emphasis of techniques destroys man and cultivate capacity and efficiency without understanding life. To stuff the child with a lot of information just to make him qualify the examinations is an unintelligent form of education. The right education should help you to find out for yourself, what you really with all your heart, love to do.

Krishnamurthy advocated four aims of education.

1. Development of integrated whole personality: Education is not acquiring knowledge, it is to see the significance of life as a whole. The purpose of education is to create human beings who are integrated.
2. Freedom: The purpose of education is to integrate men and women of freedom, intense psychological freedom. He says, freedom is not the purpose/aim of education, it is education itself.

3. Development of self-knowledge: Only through self-knowledge could truth be determined. Self-awareness provides the necessary clarity of vision to determine what is true. Understanding of the self is the basis of all understanding. Krishnamurthy denied the knowledge, which is not based on self-knowledge. So, the purpose of education is to see the development of the self in each and every individual.
4. Development of love towards and right relationship with others: Everything is relational so there is no existence without relationship.

The purpose of education is to cultivate right relationship based on love and compassion. Love and right relationship emanate from proper understanding of the self. The individual who understands his own self in its totality can relate himself with others properly.

For achieving the aims of education, he conceived a curriculum based on the appreciation for the environment, art, music and aesthetic in addition to traditional subjects. In 1928, he established the Rishi Valley Education Centre. The Krishna Murthy Foundation of India was established for setting educational institutions. The work of the foundation includes education, research and environmental programmes that are conducted in overall perspective deriving from Krishna Murthy's thoughts, the schools work for development of both academic knowledge and skills as well as psychological development of the children. Some schools under the foundation are working for the children from underprivileged and lower middle class backgrounds. The learning approach adopted includes exploration and discovery and quality interaction between teachers and students. There are a variety of co-curricular activities and programmes that engage students creatively in their immediate environment.

Gijubhai Bhadeka

Gijubhai Bhadeka was an inspiring educationist and teacher who rejected the orthodox system of school teaching and instituted playful mechanisms for learning and used Montessori methods of teaching, especially in language arts. Bhadeka was a proponent of the Montessori philosophy of childhood education. He started Dakshionmurthy Vinay Mander and the school followed his teaching method. Gijubhai worked with children in the village context, teaching them history, geography and other subjects in a way that appeal and be relevant. His book Divaswapna gives a picture of how an inspired teacher can introduce meaningful education even in an ordinary school.

4

Western Educational Thinkers on Alternative Education

Great western educational thinkers have been reiterating that there is a need to bring a revolution in the world of education. Most of them were against the conventional education system and the supremacy of the church and religion. The major educational thinkers who fought for the education were:

Ivan D Illich

Ivan Illich was against the conventional institutions and criticised the structure, function and purpose of the school. He says,

> *School is anti-educational*: It (school) rejects the outside school learning as non-education. Discouraging other institutions which provide knowledge and making education as impersonal activity, this is bureaucratic structure and detached from day to day reality. *School is divisive institution*: School introduces a kind of division in the society. There are different types of schools, special curricula, and separate classes. Only a few reaches the top of the educational pyramid and some others feel inferior and it leads them to drop outs.
>
> *School alienates an individual*: official ideology of the school is to liberate the child from the clutches of ignorance. But in reality, the consciousness of the child through psychic manipulation and makes him/her a mere knowledge consumer. School does not give any chance to enjoy the schooling. School have alienated child from his/her learning and also from self-activity.
>
> *School as an institution of political manipulation*: School in its origin is a political rather than educational institution, it means serving the interest of the dominant political ideology of the nation. But in the view of Illich, school as political is distinct, unique and all pervasive.

According to Illich proposed educational system needs participatory, decentralised and liberating technology and a radically altered vision of social relations. So, he argued for de-schooling of society. This will happen only through the restructuring of educational relationship between learner and environment. For this, he advocated some goals for educational revolution. These are:

- To liberate access to things by abolishing the control which persons and institutions now exercise over their education value.
- To liberate the sharing of skills by guaranteeing freedom to teach or exercise them on request.
- To liberate the critical and creative resources of people by returning to individual persons the ability to call and hold meetings, an ability now increasingly monopolised by institutions which claim to speak for people.
- To liberate the individual from the obligation to shape his expectations to the services offered by an established profession by providing him with the opportunity to draw on the experience of his peers and to entrust himself to the teacher, guide, advisor or healer of his choice.

He understood the educative value of modern technology to build his educational alternatives. He said that properly controlled technology could provide each man with the ability to understand his environment better and shape it powerfully with his own hands. Therefore, he says, some approaches for achieving real learning. These are:

- *Reference services to educational objectives*: In schooled society, schools have monopolised educational materials. Simple educational objects have been expensively packaged by the knowledge industry. This monopoly of things by the school creates radical scarcity and access to things is denied radically. In de-schooled society, reference services to educational objects will liberate the things from the school and make them accessible to everyone.
- *Skill exchange:* In schooled society, due to the certification effect skilled teachers are very rare. De-schooling makes use of skill models effectively and ushers in free flow of skills, and the freedom of universal skill exchange is guaranteed. Discrimination in skill demonstration and skill exchange on the basis of education pedigree is disestablished. Skilled teachers are provided with opportunity to list their skills and they are willing to serve as models for others who want to learn these skills and addresses at which they can be reached.
- *Peer matching:* This is most important thing of Illich's alternative educational institution. Peer group is one of the basic and dynamic educational resources. Free flow of feelings and thoughts takes place only in peer group. Schooled society virtually restricts peer matching, they provide opportunity only in institutionalised meetings and obligatory assemblies. But in de-schooling, providing the young from their earliest age with invitation to meet, evaluate and seek out others would prepare them for lifelong interest in seeking new partners for new endeavours.
- *Reference services to education at large:* In school society, teachers are considered as pedagogic therapists, knowledge capitalists and secular priests, their prime function is to school the consciousness

of the child. But in de-school, independent educators would replace these school teachers.

According to Illich, skill exchange and peer matching reduces the negative effects of school and realise the democratic ideals of education for all. De-schooling alternatives include learning webs with a view to liberate the education and opportunity networks consisting of multiple channels of learning exchanges.

The Illich typology of educators may be differentiated into three categories.

1. *Educational administrators*: Educational administrators will be technicians and architects, who will create and operate the various educational networks. With an understanding of knowledge, society and people, educational administers will know how to detect barriers to relevant information and how to eliminate these barriers. Of paramount importance is the stipulation that these individuals know how to stay out of the learner's way and in no way direct or determine his studies. Basically the role of the proposed administrator will be to provide the tools necessary for any educational adventure.
2. *Pedagogical counsellors*: The pedagogical counsellors will serve as guides. While the administrators will be primarily concerned with the technology necessary for operation of the educational network, these guides will focus on individualised educational programmes. Prospective learners will designate their goals and the counsellors will help them to find the path to these goals. The pedagogical counsellor will also diagnose educational difficulties and prescribe effective remedies. In addition, these individuals will not have to suppress their opinions and values in favour of their clients but instead would be free to make value judgements because clients will also be free.
3. *Educational leader*: The educational leader of initiator appears to be the weakest link in the Illich typology. The functions proposed for these educators are massive and at times, vague. The educational leaders will be required to discover, reveal and proclaim the truth that could set men free. Illich claims that the activities of educational initiators would be luxuries, forms of leisure and meaningful exercises both for the leaders and their followers. To those tasks the requirement that these individuals be able to be questioned and then to answer in such a way as to provoke ever deeper questions.

When Illich speaks of education, he refers to a lifelong process which is more adult than child centred. In fact they see childhood as being a creation of the school. The programmes for de-schooling has two assumptions: (1) control of modern societies must be switched from manipulative or authoritarian institutions to convivial or democratic ones; (2) the school which is manipulative institution, is being and should be replaced.

John Dewey

Dewey criticised the schooling at his time, he said that education is divorced from life and it eliminates its unworthy and obsolescent features. According to him, school is extended to individual's social environment. His thoughts are related to three words; Thinking, Experiencing and Education. His educational prescriptions are based on his views on how we think. Thinking does not occur in isolation, without experience or action. Thinking is a method of intelligent experiencing and it is connected with the increase of efficiency in action. These experiences serve for education. Experience and education are not separate; experience is education. Education is the process of reconstruction of experience. In the words of Dewey,

> "An ounce of experience is better than a ton of theory". And he says, Education is life itself and not a preparation for life."

According to Dewey, there are two fundamental factors in the educational process. They are individual and the social factors, both of them are equally important. Child as the central part of the education process and education starts based on the abilities, capacities and nature of the student and also it is suitable for the social context of the child. Dewey said that we can't separate the individual from the society because both of them exist at the same time. In education, social factor is the basic one and education emphasises the socialisation and social consciousness of the race.

Dewey suggested the educational aims which must be founded upon the needs and intrinsic activities of the student. And they need an environment which helps to liberate and organise their abilities and the aim of education must be clear and specific. According to him, there are three types of educational aims: natural development aim, social efficiency aim and cultural aim. In the natural development aim, education fixes attention to the physical and mental health of the student and also understands the individual differences. The second aim, social efficiency aim, brings out the natural abilities of the individual in occupation having social meaning. This aim indicates the importance of industrial competency, civic efficiency and good citizenship. The cultural aim indicates the cultivation of mind of the people with respect to appreciation of ideas, art and broad human interests.

The generic method of education for Dewey was the scientific method, which he believed that it could be applied to all areas of human inquiry by adopting problem solving. He outlined the essentials of problem solving, these are:

(1) the pupil has a genuine situation of experience;
(2) a genuine problem develops within this situation as a stimulus of thought;
(3) he possesses the information and makes the observation needed to deal with it;

(4) solutions occur to him,
(5) he has opportunity and occasion to test his ideas by application to make their meaning clear and discover for himself their validity.

Dewey was dissatisfied with the existing educational system and school. To test his educational ideas in practice to touch in real life, he established a Laboratory school at Chicago University in 1986. Here we could see a smooth transition from outside knowledge to school knowledge and establish continuity between them. Dewey provided real life experiences of home and community in school. He believed that "the first approach to any subject in school should be as non-scholastic as possible." To realise what an experience or empirical situation means one has to engage in the sort of occupation that interest and engage activity in ordinary life. This school was also a response to the demands of the industrial society and democratic policy. So, he crafted all programmes in school essentially around activity. He outlined three stages of elementary school:

1. Play period (Up to 4 to 8 years): In this period, children begin to come out of the limits of home life and make acquaintance with the social world. Here they distinguish between means and ends.
2. Period of Spontaneous attention (8 to 12 years): This is the period where children would be able to willing to acquire different forms of skills. Here they understand the difference between means and ends.
3. Period of Reflective attention (12 onwards): In these periods, children adequately master the methods of thought, enquiry and activity and are able to raise problems for themselves to seek solutions.

Laboratory school is a craft centred school, consisted of and offered vocations like carpentry, metallurgy, tailoring, embroidery, smithy, etc.

Bertrand Russell

Russell lived in an era where education and life at large were under the authority of the church. He protested against the restriction of the church. He opposed the religion because it imposes some doubtful things in the minds of the children. He opposed the control of education by church because it undermines the intellectual virtues of toleration and impartiality and only contributes to prejudice, religious bigotry and bias. He was also against the state-controlled education as it produces docile and uncritical citizens.

In his principle of social constructivism, he points out education as a political institution which develops conformity among the students to preserve the statues quo. According to him, education is the strongest force on the side of what exists and against fundamental changes. He says all education has a political motive, it aims at strengthening some group, national or religious or even social, in competition with other groups. In Russell's view development of person with ideal character should be the aim of education. He identifies four universal characteristics, which are the bases of ideal character and jointly constitute the aim of education, these are:

1. *Vitality*: It is more psychological than a mental characteristic and presumably always present where there is perfect health. Vitality is present in all vigorous children. However, school tends to diminish it. Russel believes that where vitality exists there is feeling of pleasure. Vitality heightens pleasure and it tends to diminish pain. So, preservation and development of vitality should be one of the aims of education.
2. *Courage*: According to Russel, courage is a precious virtue of human beings. It is the combination of self-respect with an impersonal outlook on life. So, everyone should become courageous. Also, he said that there are two types of fears, rational and irrational fears. Rational fears are desirable and irrational fears are undesirable. When there is courage, there is absence of irrational fears. He says, all men and women can be so educated as to enable them to live without irrational fears and fear operates at the personal and social levels. He commented that state, church and herd use social disapproval to develop irrational fears in the individual. Therefore, Russell assigns education the aim of developing courage among the children so as to overcome irrational fear.
3. *Sensitiveness*: It is the third constituent of Russell's aim of education. It is related to our emotions. Sensitiveness or love is more than sympathy for other human beings. Sympathy is a psychological trait shown for near and dear. Sensitiveness moves beyond this kind of physical or concrete sympathy and enlarges itself to include physically unrelated and distant human beings to identify with their sufferings. Russell calls this as abstract sympathy. The failure to feel abstract sympathy leads to exploiting of backward people, condoning of war, ignoring of diseases, poverty death, etc. Russell believes that education has to develop true sensitiveness among children.
4. *Intelligence*: According to Russell, intelligence includes both knowledge and receptivity to knowledge. Intelligence demands as alert curiosity and genuine love of knowledge. He says that there are a number of intellectual virtues that should be cultivated, because they are essential for the successful pursuit of knowledge. He mentioned the following virtues:
   - Curiosity: It is not only a necessary trait but the most fundamental trait for intellectual development.
   - Open mindedness: It is a prerequisite for knowledge acquisition and it is the quality that goes along with genuine desire for knowledge.

- Belief: One must have faith in knowledge acquisition and this faith must be inculcated among children.
- Perseverance: It increases the spirit of knowledge perseverance among children.
- Patience: Patience refers to the continuous and restless effort to get over difficulties. It is necessary requirement for intellectual development.
- Concentration: The power of concentration is valuable provided it is within the control of the will. It is especially the control of attention in the face of distraction.
- Exactness: Three kinds of exactness are needed for intellectual development. They are muscular accuracy, aesthetic accuracy and logical accuracy.

Russell advocated a stage-wise scheme of education. There are three stages. The first stage is starting with Nursery school education of the Montessori type. The second is General education stage and this stage includes the children between the ages of 6 to 14. This stage enables the individual to discover his/her special aptitudes in which he/she get specialised later. The subjects of this stage are reading, dancing, geography, history, modern language, literature, mathematics, science, classics outdoor activities and hygiene. Later years stage is the third one, which involves those who wish to specialise in general scholastic education — Classics, Mathematics and Science — and for those who wish to prolong all-round education.

Russell established a model school based on his ideas known as Beacon Hill School. This stands for Russell's response to the evils of the prevailing British system of schooling. His own children are the inmates of this school. Here education of the children is done in an environment of love and knowledge. Children are never urged to go through any subject; they wait till they saw some reason for their wish to learn a subject. They do a great deal of nature study. Not a single method of teaching is followed in the school, but at the same time, methods include projects and vocations, which are adapted to each child's special ability. There is self-government which works through a student council, where everything was discussed by and with the children

Paulo Freire

Critical pedagogy was influenced by the works of Paulo Freire, the most celebrated critical educator. Critical pedagogy has its roots in the critical theory of the Frankfurt School, whose influence is evident in the emancipator works of Paulo Freire. According to him, liberatory education focuses on the development of critical consciousness, which enables learners to recognise connections between their individual problems and experiences and the social contexts in which they are embedded. Coming to consciousness is the necessary first step of "Praxis", configured as ongoing, reflective approach to taking action. Praxis involves engaging in a cycle of theory, application, evaluation, reflection and then back to theory. Social transformation is the product of praxis at the collective level.

Postmodern, feminist, anti-racist, postcolonial and queer theories have all played a role in expanding and transforming Freirean critical pedagogy, shifting its predominant focus on class to include categories such as race, gender, sexuality, ethnicity, nationality and age. In place of the Marxist meta narrative and essentialist categories upon which Freire's vision of liberatory education relies, many contemporary critical pedagogues have adopted more postmodern, anti-essentialist conceptions of identity, language and power, while at the same time retaining the Freirean emphasis on critique, disrupting oppressive regimes of power/knowledge and social change.

Banking Concept of Education: Positions students are considered to be as empty vessels to be filled by the teacher. According to Paulo Freire in Pedagogy of the Oppressed, education is traditionally framed as an act of depositing, in which the students are the depositories and the teacher lectures and the students receive, memorise and repeat. Freire explains that banking education is generally characterised by the following oppressive attitudes and practices.

- The teacher teaches and the students are taught
- The teacher knows everything and the students know nothing
- The teacher thinks and the students are thought about
- The teacher talks and the students are disciplined
- The teacher chooses and enforces his choice and the students comply
- The teacher acts and the students have the illusion of acting through the action of the teacher
- The teacher chooses the programme content and the students adapt to it
- The teacher confuses the authority of knowledge with his own professional authority, which he sets in opposition to the freedom of the students
- The teacher is the subject of the learning process while the pupils are mere objects.

Consicentisation: It refers to learning to perceive social, political and economic contradictions — developing a critical awareness — so that individuals can take action against the oppressive elements of reality of the oppressed.

Constructivism: Constructivism is the philosophy that views learning as an active process in which learners construct their own understanding and knowledge of the world through action and reflection. Constructivist argues that individuals generate rules and mental models as the result of their experiences with both other human subjects and their environments and in turn use these rules and models to make sense of new experiences.

Three important concepts emerged from this definition are:

1. Knowledge is socially constructed. It is not something that exists outside of language and the social subjects who use it. Learning — obtaining knowledge and making meaning — is thus a social process rather than the work of the isolated individual mind, it cannot be divorced from learner's social context.
2. Learning is an active process. Students learn by doing rather than by passively absorbing information.
3. Knowledge is constructed from experience. Students bring prior knowledge into a learning situation, which in turn forms the basis of their construction of new knowledge. Upon encountering something new, learners must first reconcile it in some way with their previous ideas and experiences. This may mean changing what they believe, expanding their understanding or disregarding the new information as irrelevant.

In this framework the learning is not a process of transmission of information from teacher to student model which positions the student as a passive receptacle but an active process of construction on the part of the learner that involves making meaning out of a multiplicity stimulus. In practice, educators use active techniques to introduce students to information and issues and then encourage students to reflect on and talk about what they did and how their understanding is changing. The teacher makes sure she understands the student's pre-existing conceptions and guides activities to address and build on them. Constructivism also often utilises collaboration and peer criticism as a way of facilitating student's abilities to reach a new level of understanding.

Some concepts introduced by Paulo Freire with modern critical educators are:

- *Culture Circle*: A discussion group is the one in which educators use representations and themes from learner's everyday lives to initiate critical dialogue regarding the various factors that contribute to the real material, social and political contexts in which the learners are embedded. Through dialogue and collective reflection, the group of learners transforms their various observations and opinions into critical knowledge.
- *Culture of Silence*: A characteristic of oppressed people in colonised countries who do not have a voice in their society. The dominant culture silences the oppressed through the cultural transmission of discourses in schools and other institutions that support its hegemony and through ignoring or demonising other discourses that might challenge its authority. As a result, oppressed people learn to internalise negative images of them. Because they are not taught the tools of critical inquiry that would allow them to challenge these false representations, they remain passive and silent.

- *Dialogical Method*: The dialogical approach to learning abandons the lecture format and the banking approach to education in favour of dialogue and open communication among students and teachers. According to Paulo Freire, in this method, all teach and all learn. The dialogical approach contrasts with the anti-dialogical method, which positions the teacher as the transmitter of knowledge, a hierarchical framework that leads to domination and oppression through the silencing of student's knowledge and experiences.
- *Humanisation*: For Paulo Freire, the vocation of each individual is to become more fully human, configured as emancipation from oppression. Libratory education works in the service of humanity's historical vocation to become more fully human by affirming and empowering students as "subjects of decision". Humanisation is thwarted by the forces of "dehumanisation", which oppress human beings and limit their freedom. The oppressed must learn to liberate them and in turn their oppressors, who are also dehumanised through the very process of oppressing others.
- *Liberatory Education*: Liberatory education raises student's consciousness, preparing them to engage in large social struggles for liberation. It attempts to empower learners to critique and challenge oppressive social conditions and to envision and work towards a more just society.
- *Praxis*: A complete activity involving a cycle theory, application, evaluation, reflection and then back to theory. Social transformation is the product of praxis at the collection level.
- Problem Posing Education: Rejects banking education or education as the process of transferring information and embraces a view of education as consisting of acts of cognition that takes place through dialogue. Students and teachers become critical co-investigators in dialogue with each other. According to Freire, with problem posing education, 'no one teaches another, nor is anyone self-taught. Men teach each other, mediated by the world, by the cognizable objects which in banking education are owned by the teacher.'

Pierre Bourdieu

Pierre Bourdieu was a French sociologist, anthropologist and a philosopher. His major contributions are related to sociology of education. Bourdieu routinely sought to connect his theoretical ideas with empirical research. His work observes the semi-independent role of educational and cultural resources in the expression of agency. This makes his work amenable to liberal-conservative scholarships positing the fundamental cleavages of society as amongst disorderly factions of the working class, in need of disciplinary intervention where they have assumed excessive privilege. Bourdieu's most significant work is on cultural reproduction. It is a very broad understanding of culture, in line with the tradition of classical sociology, including science, law and religion as well as expressive aesthetic activities such as art, literature and music. Major terms coined by him is related to cultural reproduction are habitus, capital and field.

Theory of Habitus

Bourdieu developed a theory of the action, around the concept of habitus, which exerted a considerable influence in the social sciences. This theory seeks to show that social agents develop strategies which are adapted to the structure of the social worlds that they inhabit. These strategies are unconscious and act on the level of bodily logic. In Bourdieu's view, each relatively autonomous field of modern life ultimately engenders a specific complex of social relations where the agents will engage their everyday practice. Through this practice, they develop a certain *disposition* for social action that is conditioned by their position in the field. Disposition can be defined as a sense of game, a partly rational but partly intuitive understanding of fields and social order in general, a practice sense, a practical reason giving rise to opinions, tastes, tone of voice, typical body movements and mannerisms and so on. This disposition combined with every other disposition the individual develops through their engagement with other fields operating within the social world, will eventually come to constitute a system of dispositions, i.e., habitus, lasting, acquired schemes of perception, thought and action.

Habitus is somewhat reminiscent of some pre-existing sociological concepts such as socialisation, though it also differs from the more classic concepts in several key ways. The central aspect of the habitus is its embodiment. Habitus does not only or even primarily function at the level of explicit discursive consciousness. The internal structures become embodied and work in a deeper practical and often pre-reflexive way. For example, muscle memory cultivated in many areas of physical education. Consider the way we catch a ball — the complex geometric trajectories are not calculated, it is not an intellectual process. Although it is a skill that requires learning, it is more a physical than a mental process and has to be performed physically to be learned.

Though not deterministic, the inculcation of the subjective structures of the habitus can be observed through statistical data, for example while its selective affinity with the objective structures of the social world explains the continuity of the social order through time. As the individual habitus is always a mix of multiple engagements in the social world through the person's life, while the social fields are put into practice through the agency of the individuals, no social field or order can be completely stable. In other words, if the relation between individual predisposition and social structure is far stronger than common sense tends to believe, it is not a perfect match.

Field Theory

A field can be described as any historical, non-homogeneous social-spatial arena in which people manoeuvre and struggle in pursuit of desirable resources. And it is referred to any setting in which agents and their social positions are located. Accordingly, the position of each particular agent in the field is a result of interaction between the specific rules of the field: agents, habitus and capital. Fields interact with each other and are hierarchical. Most are subordinate to the larger field of power and class relations.

Social activity differences lead to various, relatively autonomous, social spaces in which competition centres around particular capital. These fields are treated on a hierarchical basis — with economic power usually governing — where the dynamics of fields arise out of the struggle of social actors trying to occupy the dominant positions within the field. For Bourdieu, a sociologically informed view of an artist ought to describe their relations to the field of production and their attitudes to their relations to the field of consumption. For example, a work of literature may not adequately be analysed either as the product of the author's life and beliefs which means, the subject of a work is a habitus in relationship with a 'post', a position, that is within a field. And he also revealed that, cultural revolutions are always dependent on the possibilities present in the positions inscribed in the field.

Relation between Field Theory and Habitus Theory

The methodological and theoretical concepts of habitus and field make an epistemological break with the prominent objective — subjective antinomy of the social sciences. Habitus and field are proposed to do so. The individual agents develop these dispositions in response to the objective conditions it encounters. Bourdieu theorises the inculcation of objective social structures into subjective mental experience of agents. For the objective field, place requirements on its participants for membership, so to speak, within the field. Having thereby absorbed objective social structure into a personal set of cognitive and somatic dispositions and the subjective structures of action of the agent then being commensurate with the objective structures and extent exigencies of the social field, a doxic relationship emerges.

Doxa refers to the learned, fundamental, deep founded, unconscious beliefs and values taken as self-evident universals that inform an agent's actions and thoughts within a particular field. Doxa tends to favour the particular social arrangement of the field, thus privileging the dominant and taking their position of dominance as self-evident and universally favourable. Therefore, the categories of understanding and perception that constitute a habitus, being congruous with the objective organisation of the field, tend to reproduce the very structures of the field. A doxic situation may be thought of as a situation characterised by a harmony between the objective, external structures and the subjective internal structures of the habitus. In the doxic state, the social world is perceived as natural, taken for granted and even commonsensical.

Bourdieu sees habitus as an important factor contributing to social reproduction, because it is central to generating and regulating the practices that make up social life. Individuals want to learn what conditions make possible for them, and not to aspire to what is not available to them. The conditions, in which the individual lives, generate dispositions compatible with these conditions and in a sense pre-adapted to their demands. The most improbable practices are therefore excluded as unthinkable by a kind of immediate submission to order that inclined agents to make a virtue of necessity, which is to refuse what is categorically denied and to will the inevitable.

Habitus and field can only exist in relation to each other. Although a field is constituted by the various social agents participating in it, a habitus, in effect, represents the transposition of objective structures of the field into the subjective structures of action and thought of their agent. The relationship between habitus and field is twofold. First, the field exists only in so far as social agents possess the dispositions and set of perceptual schemata that are necessary to constitute that field and imbue it with meaning. Concomitantly, by participating in the field, agents incorporate into their habitus the proper know-how that will allow them to constitute the field. Habitus manifests the structures of the field, and the field mediates between habitus and practice. Bourdieu attempts to use the concepts of habitus and field to remove the division between the subjective and the objective. He asserts that any research must be composed of two "minutes", the first minute is an objective stage of research — where one looks at the relations of the social space and the structure of the field; while the second minute must be a subjective analysis of social agents' dispositions to act and their categories of perception and understanding that result from their inhabiting the field. Bourdieu argues that proper research cannot do without these two.

Capital Theory

According to Bourdieu capital refers to the set of actually usable resources and powers. Capital is accumulated over time, plays a significant role in producing and reproducing profits in an individual's life opportunities and is most valued when it is scarce. Maintaining the structure and functioning of the social world can only be understood by taking into account all forms of capital. Bourdieu distinguishes three fundamental forms of capital: economic, cultural and social.

- *Economic Capital:* Economic capital is directly convertible into money and may be manifested in family income and wealth. Bourdieu recognises economic capital as one form of capital that is necessary to understand the social world. He actually does not pay specific attention to economic capital believing that its absence does not necessarily hinder the possession of all other forms of capital and that economic capital is insufficient in itself to understand how advantages in an individual's life opportunities are produced and reproduced.
- *Cultural Capital:* Cultural capital has been defined as symbolic resources or goods that are transmitted from generation to generation

among the middle and upper classes in order to maintain class status. According to him, there are three kinds of cultural capital:

1. embodied cultural capital refers to manifestations of individual appreciations of cultural goods through their actions and style;
2. objectified cultural capital refers to the cultural goods themselves such as art works, books and instruments;
3. institutionalised cultural capital entails forms of objectification such as educational credentials.

Earlier Bourdieu argues that family is the primary place where children acquire cultural capital. Parents pass it on to their children through talking and behaviour. Elite class children inherit more cultural capital because elite class parents have more cultural capital and are more capable of teaching it to their children. Elite families have greater socio economic capital to support children to acquire cultural capital such as art and music. Elite class parents have more free time available with their children to transmit cultural capital. The positive effect of cultural capital on education achievement is derived from two aspects. First, school education is essentially a "symbolic violence", teachers as agents of the elite, evaluate students based on elite cultural standards. Secondly, this culture is monopolised by the elite but is not directly taught to students in schools. As a result, only students from elite families can master and perform elite cultural capital in daily activities and teacher student communication, which means they obtain better teacher evaluations. In this sense, cultural capital is the most valuable relation to education and it is the most relevant to one's academic success.

- *Social capital:* Social capital is the sum of the resources, actual or virtual, that accrue to an individual or a group by virtue of possessing a durable network of more or less institutionalised relationships of mutual acquaintance and recognition. In order for individuals to gain such capital they must work for it consistently and it takes time according to Bourdieu. For some families, cultural capital is accumulated over a period of generations as they adopt cultural investment strategies and pass them on to their children. This gives children an opportunity to realise their potential through education and they pass on those same values to their children. Over time, individuals in such families gain cultural currency which gives them an inherent advantage over other groups of people, which is why there is such variation in academic achievement in children of different social classes.

Education as Cultural Reproduction

Cultural reproduction is a concept developed by Bourdieu. Cultural reproduction is the mechanism by which existing cultural forms, values, practices and shared understandings are transmitted from one generation to another and thereby sustaining the continuity of cultural experiences across time. It is also a process by which aspects of culture are passed on from person to person or from society to society. Cultural reproduction often results in social reproduction or the process of transferring aspects of society inter-generationally. In different ways it has happened. Popular groups of people, different social classes may act to reproduce the existing social structure so as to preserve their advantage. Otherwise the processes of schooling in modern societies are the important mechanisms of cultural reproduction, and do not operate solely through what is taught in courses of formal instruction. In olden days, people have moved from different regions for their livelihood, during this time they absorbed certain cultural norms and traditions. People learn these things in an informal way while they are out of home. The process of transfer of accepted cultural norms, values and information are known as socialisation.

Other two terms related to cultural reproduction are enculturation and diffusion. Enculturation means a partly conscious and unconscious learning experience when the older generation invites, induces and compels the younger generation to adopt traditional ways of thinking and behaving. In different ways, enculturation duplicates the norms and traditions of previous generations. Diffusion is the dispersion of cultural norms and behaviours between otherwise unrelated groups or individuals. Parents and teachers are the most influential enculturation forces of cultural reproduction

Education determines an individual's social status, class, values and hierarchy. The role of education in cultural reproduction is through the distribution of cultural capital. This notion of cultural capital accumulation and the degree to which an individual attains cultural capital determines the individual's access to resources and opportunities. The concept of education as an agent of cultural reproduction is done through hidden curriculum, which refers to the materials indirectly. This refers to the socialisation aspects of education process. Here students acquire appropriate attitudes and values needed to further succeed within the confines of education. A student's success or failure within the formal education system is a function to demonstrate both measures of formal educational qualifications as well as the attainment of the aforementioned qualities acquired through socialisation mechanisms. This nature of education reproduced throughout all stages of the system, from primary to higher education. One's ability to successfully complete the process of educational attainment strongly correlates to the capacity to realise adequate pay, occupational prestige, social status etc. upon work force participation.

Education System as Capitalist System

Education reflects the capital system; it differentiates the individuals and assigns them the skills necessary to fulfil their destined occupation. An individual is provided with the appropriate attitude that should be observed within the labour force. Further, it establishes an acceptance to the reproduction of submissive attitude to the established order. The primary role of education is to sort individuals rather than equally educating those with high levels of accumulated social capital from parents or other sources who are more easily able to excel within the system of education. Thus, these individuals will continue on a track that places them into specialised and comparatively highly prestigious occupations. In disparity, those with social or cultural capital will maintain low levels throughout the process of education and be placed into occupations with little demand for cultural capital significantly less specialised and prestigious occupation. With this occupational selection, both the individuals will maintain the cultural norms and social status associated with each outside of their occupations as well.

By considering the intrinsic value of education or the externally perceived value, each unit of educational attainment requires foregone earnings to attain. In so much as an individual would have to sacrifice wages in order to gain an additional unit of education. Outside the foregone monetary earnings, there are also direct expenses such as tuition, stationery, books etc. When acquiring education one must consider the less direct psychic costs. With this if there is an economic consideration and trade, an individual must consider it in their further education aspiration. One who has resources and the desire to continue education has a significant comparative advantage than who does not. This financial aspect of educational acquirement proves yet another consideration in the reproductive nature of education.

One who successfully completes the process of educational attainment incurs a significant comparative advantage over a similar individual who does not. Thus, the degree to which education reproduces cultural and social norms already present in the underlying society stands to prove a significant factor in the continued propagation of these established norms. With this harsh division between individuals who do and do not complete the process of formal education, social stratification and inequality between the two groups emerges. This further confirms cultural norms and reproduces the same system upon each successive generation.

N F S Grundtvig

Nikolai Frederik Severin Grundtvig was a philosopher, poet, theologian, educator, historian and a social critic. However, education was one of his primary concerns. Grundtvig believed that the classical education of the time with an emphasis on Greek and Latin studies, created a rift between life and learning. His particular concern was that schools should bring dignity to rural people and to the life of the farmer, the majority of the Denmark's population at that time. He wanted education to instil a pride in national culture and a love of learning that would be lifelong. For Grundtvig, to be a human being is to accept and take pride in one's community connection and cultural identity. His philosophy of learning was based on an understanding of human identity that includes an individual identity cannot be separated from community, and the wholeness of the individual happens in the connection with the community.

Grundtvig encouraged placing our human identity at the core of education. In the 1830's Grundtvig carried out a tireless mission to convince the Danish population that a new kind of school was critical if Denmark was to have a successful transition to democracy.

Since the kind of school envisioned by Grundtvig did not exist, they would have to be created. These schools would embrace the concepts of enlightenment and folklighted. Grundtvig in fact, hoped these universities would achieve enlightenment through folk lighted and thus called his vision *folkeojskoler*. In these folk high schools, students would be encouraged to bloom rather than be educated to conform. The educational operative of encouragement, the living word, would foster three important interplays: teacher-student, student-student, national poet-educational community.

1. *Teacher-student interplay:* Since the Grundtvigion classroom would revolve around competency in life rather than around scholarship, teachers would need more than a thorough knowledge of some subject. They must exhibit nourishing attitudes, an energetic spirit and dialogical behaviour. It would fall upon them to fan each student's spark of life into a flame of vital force through enthusiastic encouragement and give and take discussion as equals. In earlier times, Grundtvig strongly believed in the necessity of teacher vitality and also he said we must select the liveliest possible people as teachers. Lecturers mostly must be discarded because students were there not only to be taught by teachers but to teach their instructors in turn. "Reciprocal teaching" was Grundtvig's idea of the ideal learning process.
2. *Student-student interplay*: Students would not remain in folk high schools throughout their lives. Therefore, it was important to Grundtvig that they learn to carry on the kind of dialogue among themselves that they heard modelled by their enlightened teachers. Without this extension of application, the real world of the students would not be engaged. Further, since people differ in beliefs and behaviour, Grundtvig was an advocate of diversity in student body make up to broaden the range of dialogue. This notion was radical to his contemporaries because it encouraged mixing of poor and rich, men and women of all ages.
3. *National poet-educational community interplay*: Depth as well as breadth of enlightenment was necessary to cultivate a student from partial bloom to full blossom. As a poet, Grundtvig knew the difficulty of trying to search the inner recesses of one's being, nevertheless, only this interpersonal scrutiny could confirm a person's self-appreciation. By poetry, then he means a therapeutic and not necessarily aesthetic exchange with oneself. Poetry would reveal how a personal interpretation of life and ways of communications are necessary in

order to intervene and allay the doubts in men's minds that result in despair. To model this poetic process, national poets should visit the folk high schools. Their insight and eloquence would rejuvenate the folk school mission, enlightenment of life through the living word and would encourage interpersonal communication in the students.

Folk High School

Grundtvig postulated a folk high school model consisting of at least eight distinct features:

- Subject matter would not be significant; most important would be if both, teacher and students, are interested in whatever they choose for study.
- Dialogue should be the tool of instructional communication.
- No tests, grades or degree would be imposed on students.
- Duration of a student's stay would be limited to one term of three to four months (usually), or two consecutive terms (on rare occasions).
- Students must live in the school during the term.
- Students would work together on some form of physical enterprise.
- Each term's educational community would be self-governing.
- Teachers would stay at the folk high school along with the students.

A folk school with these features would help students to learn affective and cognitive principles useful in life. At such an educational institution, active contemplation and reflective action would be merged, the enlightened life would be encouraged through the living word, and people's lives would be enriched and set free. Throughout their lives people could return to folk high schools, as either student or teacher, to reinvigorate their sense of self.

Grundtvg did not actually found any schools. His philosophy was put into practice by Christen Kold and was based on a deep faith in the intrinsic abilities of all individuals and a belief that education should be available to everyone. "Schools for Life" as Grundtvig called them were to assist people by understanding their own identity and to strengthen and empower communities. The folk schools were part of a decentralised grass root movement that gave farmers a means for personal and social transformation. Almost 50 folk schools were started in Denmak following Grundtvig's inspiration. Christen Kold founded the first folk school with some fundamental beliefs:

- Education must consider the nature of children and youth and their needs
- Students must be given time to develop the capacity for feeling facts and appreciation before learning skills
- The living word (oral cultural) is central
- The wholeness of the individual was experienced only in the context of the community

- The purpose of education was to respond to the needs and struggles of common people
- Education should embrace heart, mind and body. The main purpose of education was not to teach factual knowledge, but "life awakening". The school should be for life, for the spiritual and for that which is of the heart
- The school should be free of government control and there should be no tests, grades or certificates of competence given.

Folk schools model as an educational approach that places relationship, culture and personal and community empowerment at the centre of learning and life. Grundtvig believed that cultural identity in each individual is born in a particular time and place and within a particular, historical, cultural and political context. Understanding and honouring that identity is critical. Democracy is strengthened through citizens that understand their history. They are actively engaged in dialogue, and participate in problems-solving to effect social change. This belief is borne out in the crediting of the folk school movement with Denmark's successful transition to democracy. Folk schools are not just about learning skills, but also about human empowerment and educating for participatory democracy. Steven Borish, a scholar of Grundtvig, proposes four lessons that folk schools have to offer:

1. Real education begins with the communication of a sense of personal mission and purpose, and the belief that everyone has the ability to acquire the skills and knowledge to accomplish that mission.
2. The principle of folklighted offers an alternative to nationalism. It is a form of patriotism that values culture and identify while emphasising other nations and culture.
3. Education should be for all aspects of life and lifelong.
4. The movement that gave rise to folk schools was local, decentralised and grassroots.

Folk education offers the possibility of re-visioning local life, culture and social ecology. In the United States, the philosophical and pedagogical framework that informs folk schools may also go with names such as community learning centre or cultural centre. Folk schools connect and build a myriad of community resources and they capitalise on networking and collaboration at its finest. Folk schools can provide much needed enrichment and balance to public schools during an era of enormous pressure for academic and intellectual achievement. Public school or folk school collaborations are happening in a number of folk schools. Folk schools in the United States offer:

- A local place for conscious educational experience
- Build collaborations and networks among diverse community groups or organisations

- Build a local strength
- Build appreciation of local culture and agriculture
- Encourage a recovery of local voice, empowerment and cultural memory
- Emphasise dialogue, conversation and relationships
- Offer the expression of an alternative educational paradigm, one that is collaborative and non-competitive
- Offer enrichment as well as core programming for public, private and home schools
- Provide a cortex for diverse groups to come together for shared learning
- Provide a context for the presentation and discussion of local issues
- Inspire local economic initiatives that support the local economy.

The needs of the people in a community can be different in different times and places. So a teacher meets the abilities to understand the people, there lies. Folk schools in the United States reflect a hope for making a transition from unsustainable industrial society towards sustainable, post modern societies. Denmark has demonstrated the degree to which a folk school can be woven into the fabric of society and can be a rich resource for renewal and change. Folk schools have great potential to inspire change for education and communities.

Alexander Sutherland Neill

A S Neill was a Scottish progressive educator. He is best known as an advocate of personal freedom for children and has been correspondingly criticised as an instigator of permissiveness. Neill deeply trusted in the ability of the students to direct his or her own learning. He promoted the idea that this natural ability was nurtured in freedom. Neill believed that the happiness of the child was of paramount consideration in the child's upbringing and that this happiness grew from a sense of personal freedom in the child. He felt that deprivation of this sense of freedom during childhood and all the consequent unhappiness experienced by the repressed child was responsible for most of the psychological disorder of adulthood.

According to Neill, the aim of education is to feel joy and find happiness. Other educators disagreed because even though doing fun things has been the desire of people throughout the ages, it is not the main goal of education. Education is not necessarily viewed as the means to guarantee happiness but rather education is what enables one to be equipped with the necessary knowledge to make decisions in that quest for happiness and the expertise to make things happen. Some progressive teachers may agree that when the child is young it is good not to impose any formal teaching. The fact that Neill believed in never requiring learning is one sided since this view fails to teach a child to think and act in an orderly, disciplined manner. Neill taught that the school should fit the child. However, critics have said that this concept deceives the child into thinking that life will adapt to him or her. Additionally, critics have argued that providing an environment that encourages the child to have no fear is very unrealistic and dangerous both physically and emotionally, arguing that to function effectively in the natural and social worlds the child must learn norms of behaviour. He said that limiting discipline to a minimum and allowing freedom not license and respecting the rights of others. According to him, teachers are honest and sincere toward their pupils and avoiding giving the child guilt feeling. He opposed to teach religion in school.

Neill's effect on the educational systems throughout the world was varied according to the particular time period and country. It has been said that Neill's greatest influence has been on the thinking of parents. His views on child rearing caused parents to reflect with care and concern about their children's upbringing. Neill either reinforced or provided authoritative confirmation for values and beliefs formulated by parents. Inspired of the scrutiny toward Neill's practices, it is clear that he influenced a significant number of parents to evaluate and define the way they brought up their children.

Neill has been criticised for excessive idealism and even moral indifference. His methods, some argue, do not inculcate positive values. Yet for students to govern themselves requires of them considerable moral responsibility. For students to determine their own learning gives them ownership occurred during their learning. The success of Summerhill School suggests that when Neill's methods are properly employed, teacher rises to an exceptional level of caring and involvement in the lives of their students. More than an instructor, a teacher's role becomes that of a parent. Indeed, by defining a new approach to parenting, the influence of Neill's writings spread far beyond education.

Summerhill School

Summerhill School was founded in 1921 by A S Neill, with a belief that the school should be made to fit the child, rather than the other way around. Neill founded Summerhill School with the belief that the function of a child is to live his own life not the life that his anxious parents think he should live and not a life according to the purpose of an educator who thinks he knows best. It is run as a democratic community. It is an example of both democratic education and alternative education. Summerhill School operates upon the major principles of democracy, equality and freedom. The main goals of Summerhills are:

- Allow children freedom to grow emotionally
- Give children power over their own lives
- Give children the time to develop naturally
- Create a happier childhood by removing fear and coercion by adults.

Summerhill is noted for its philosophy that children learn best with freedom from coercion. Here all lessons are optional, and pupils are free to choose what to do with their time. Classes are voluntary at Summerhill. Although most students attend, depending on their age and reasons, children choose whether to go of their own accord and without adult compulsion. This novel attendance policy, the school is based on democratic policy. Neill was more concerned with both the social and academic development of children. So they choose some important approaches to teaching. There is no concept of a year or form at Summerhills rather than children are placed according to their interest or level of understanding in a given subject. It is not uncommon for a single class to have pupils of widely varying ages or for pupils as young as 13 or 14 to take public examinations. This structure reflects that children should progress at their own pace, rather than having to meet a set standard by a certain age. Neill believed that children who were educated in this way were better prepared than traditionally educated children for most of life's changes including higher education.

Summerhill classroom was popularly assumed to reflect Neill's anti-authoritarian beliefs, but in fact classes were traditional in practice. He did not show outward interest in classroom pedagogy and was mainly interested in pupil's happiness. He did not consider lesson quality as important and thus there were no distinctive Summerhills and classroom methods. There are only two classrooms which operate on a "drop-in" basis for all or part of the day, the workshop and the art room. Anyone can come to these classrooms and with supervision make just about anything. Neill felt that the Summerhill School showed that, free from the coercion of traditional schooling, students responded with their own motivation rather than self-indulgence. He felt that children who attended Summerhills were likely to emerge with a healthy and mature scepticism towards adult society. These tendencies were perhaps all the more remarkable considering that the children accepted by Summerhill were often from problematic backgrounds, where parental conflict or neglect had resulted in children arriving in a particularly unhappy state of mind.

In addition to taking control of their own time, pupils can participate in the self- governing community of the school. School meetings are held four times in a week, where pupils and staff alike have an equal voice in the decisions that affect their day to day lives, discussing issues and creating or changing school laws. Meetings are also opportunities for the community to vote on a course of action for unresolved conflicts. There are two main methods of resolving conflicts at Summerhill. In the first instance, one should go to an Ombudsman to resolve a conflict. It is an elected committee of older members of the community, whose job it is to intervene in disputes. The second is the Tribunal, the school meeting which concerns itself with people who break the school rules. Today Summerhill School is a boarding and day school serving primary and secondary education in a democratic fashion.

Everett Reimer

Everett Reimer was born in the United States and a strong supporter of Illich and he has done too many things — sold maps, played professional football, printed greeting cards and worked in a tyre factory. After that he worked for the Atomic Energy Commission, for the Survey Research Center at the University of Michigan, and for the Washington Research Center of the Maxwell School, University of Syracuse. Later he became Secretary of the Puerto Rican Committee of Human Resources, and worked for the Alliance for Progress. He was with Ivan Illich, at the Center for Intercultural Documentation (CIDOC), and was Director of the CIDOC seminar on Alternatives in Education. In 1972, he published his famous book *'The School is Dead'*.

According to Reimer, School has become the universal church of a technological society, incorporating and transmitting its ideology, shaping men's minds to accept this ideology, and conferring social status in proportion to its acceptance. There is no question of man's rejecting technology. The question is only one of adaptation, direction and control. There may not be much time, and the only hope would seem to lie in education — the true education of free men, capable of mastering technology rather than being enslaved by it, or by others in its name. Technology can kill by poisoning the environment, by modern warfare, by over-population. It can enslave by chaining men to endless cycles of competitive consumption, by means of police states, by creating dependence on modes of production, which are not viable in the long run. There are no certain roads of escape from these dangers. There can be no road of escape at all, however, if men remain enthralled in a monolithic secular orthodoxy. Our major threat today is a worldwide monopoly in the domination of men's minds.

The School is Dead

At first Reimer felt that school was a lagging institution in an increasingly efficient technological society. He later came to see schools as providing indispensable support for a technological society which itself was not viable. The simplest way to expose the contradictions of this society is to point out that it promises unlimited progress to unlimited numbers of people. The absurdity of this claim is conceded by the recognition of the need for birth control, but birth control itself turns out to be dependent on progress. Even at present rates of growth, by the time children can be kept in school long enough for schools to have a significant impact on birth rates, the population of the world will have increased threefold. And this is using conservative projections. If modern medical techniques were made generally available, the rate of population increase would double or triple! We retain breathing space only by letting poor babies die at ten times the rate of privileged babies. During the past decade, the actual rate at which the benefits of modern institutions have been extended to the underprivileged people of the world is scarcely greater than the rate of population growth. On a per capita basis, individuals have benefited marginally, if at all.

Part of the problem lies in the inefficiency of modern institutions, including schools. The greater part lies in the promise of unlimited progress. As the world is now organised, the standard of living in India can rise only if the standard of living in the United States also rises. Yet at three per cent rise in the United States, the average income is twice the total income of the average Indian. Raising world consumption standards to US levels would multiply the combustion of fossil fuels by fifty times, the use of iron a hundred times, the use of other metals over two hundred times. By the time these levels were reached, consumption levels in the United States would again have tripled and the population of the world would also have tripled. Such projections lead to results as absurd as the premises from which they start. There can be no open-ended progress. Yet this is what schools and other modern institutions promise. This is the promise of science and technology, unrestrained by reason. This is the promise which has bred schools and other modern institutions and which they in turn propagate. Schools are an essential element of a world in which technology is king. The contradictions of such a world are becoming apparent. They are best illustrated in the school and best corrected by freeing education from the school so that people may learn the truth about the society in which they live.

For most members of the present generation, this hope that their children will benefit more from school than they get from any other means is doomed to disappointment. Schools are too expensive for this hope to be realised. For many, it may appear to be realised but the appearance will be a delusion, fostered by inflationary debasement of the academic currency. More college and high school degrees will be granted but they will mean less, both in terms of amount and kind of learning and in terms of job qualification and real income.

Most of the children in the world are not in school. Most of those who are, are dropping out as soon as possible. Most countries in the world can only afford to give their children the barest minimum of education, while the costs of schooling are everywhere rising faster than enrolments, and faster than national income. Schools are, for most people, what Remier calls 'institutional props for privilege', and yet at the same time they are the major instruments of social mobility; but at what cost in terms of true learning, true creativity, true democracy. And at what is the ultimate cost to the societies which perpetuate themselves in this way? The most urgent priority, he argues, is for a consideration of alternatives in education-alternative content, organisation, and finance. Above all, we urgently need alternative views of education itself, its nature and possible functions in the society of the future.

A N Whitehead

Alfred North Whitehead is a mathematician and a philosopher. He had some different views about education. According to him, education with inert ideas is not only useless but also harmful. He meant inert ideas that are merely received into the mind without being criticised, tested or thrown into fresh combinations. These ideas are not useful and appropriate to solve the problems in life and it should be kept alive thus preventing it from becoming inert. According to Whitehead, "Education is the acquisition of the art of the utilisation of knowledge, this is an art very difficult to impart." Once knowledge is acquired, the child should understand its application in the circumstances of his actual life and he should experience the joy of discovery. He gives importance to the understanding of an insistent present. The past knowledge equips us to present and present is a holy ground for it is the past and it is the future. According to him, knowledge is considered as the chief aim of education.

Whitehead upheld another dimension of education i.e. Wisdom. Wisdom is a way in which knowledge is held. It is related with how we handle knowledge for the determination of relevant issue and its employment to add value to our immediate experience. The only way towards wisdom is freedom in the presence of knowledge. But the only way towards knowledge is by discipline in the acquirement of ordered fact. According to him, freedom and discipline are the two essentials of education, freedom without discipline is neither liberating nor creative and discipline without freedom is ultimately futile. Undiscriminating discipline defeats its own objects by dulling the mind. The claim for freedom in education leads to the development of the whole personality.

According to Whiltehead, education is the guidance of the individual towards comprehension of the art of life and by art of life. He means the most complete achievement of varied activity expressing the potentialities of the living creature in the face of its actual environment. Each individual embodies an adventure of existence; the art of life is the guidance of the adventure.

Whitehead's another concept of education is Rhythm of education. He said it helps the development of the total personality of an individual. Rhythm of education means, it is a principle under which different subjects and modes of study should be undertaken by pupils at fitting times when they have reached the proper stages of development. He identified three rhythmic stages in the mental development.

- *Stage of romance*: This is the stage, vague apprehension of facts so knowledge is not dominated by systemic procedure.
- *Stage of precision:* Here collected facts are analysed so knowledge acquisition becomes in a systematic order.
- *Stage of generalisation:* This is the continuation of the previous stage. Fruition has been the goal of the precise training and drawing generalisations from the analysis of the collected data.

It is true that no one can complete these three stages simultaneously in all the subjects. Education should consider the individual differences among students and provide suitable one for his/her total development.

5

Curriculum in Alternative Education

In alternative education, students find spare time for fulfilling their educational objectives. So, the teaching strategies, beliefs and support services facilitate growth in academic, personal or social career development activities. Often states and communities have statutory requirements governing the number of students an alternative education programme or school can have, the type of curriculum that can be used, who can teach the programme, the length of the school day, attendance policies etc.

The curriculum offered in an alternative education programme must be academically rigorous, accessible to all students and aligned to state standards and accountability systems. The curriculum must be culturally relevant to reflect the backgrounds of the student population and is, therefore, understandable and meaningful to the students. While the academic programme is standard-based, it should not be standardised. Rather, it should be personalised for each student and instruction should be offered in a variety of learning modalities based on student's individual strengths and needs. To ensure a continual drive to success, the delivery must be data driven and real time feedback available for students and teachers.

Successful programmes have a clear focus on academic learning combined with engaging and creative instruction and a culture of high expectations for all students. Learning opportunities must provide students the knowledge and skills necessary to meet the achievement level of the next generation. Alternative programmes may choose to deliver the core content through a traditional curriculum with students earning Carnegie unit through a competency-based curriculum where students progress via mastery of learning standards. Some programmes may use a blended format where assessment can place students with prior knowledge in next level course. Alternative programmes have opportunities available for students to recover credit and accelerate learning credit recovery programmes and online course completion opportunities. Small class size and low student teacher ratios allow more rapid response when a student begins to show signs of failing Interventions, accommodations, varied learning and instructional strategies can be personalised to keep students engaged and progressing towards completion.

Teachers use a variety of effective techniques and instructional strategies to teach students with diverse learning needs, interests, background skills and prior knowledge so as to enable them to meet the state standards set for all students. Teachers modify their instructions so that the students of diverse ethnic, racial, cultural and language abilities have equal opportunity to learn through work that is challenging, interesting and related to the real-world experiences of each student. Their instruction and teaching strategies reflect their awareness of cultural differences in particular as well as those that might have an adverse affect on student learning or behaviour. Universal Design for Learning (UDL) is a model of content delivery that recognises the individuality of all learners and helps teachers adapt the curriculum to maximise individual success.

Adequate education programmes provide adequate instructional materials and resources for all students to have full and meaningful opportunities to start the standards set at the state or local levels. Instructional material and supplies are developmentally appropriate for all learners and accessible to normal students as well as students with disabilities including through a range of assistive technology services and devices

Contents of Alternative Education Curriculum

Alternative education pursues an approach which is decentralised and based on local community. This approach of education is extremely differentiated and is very much vulnerable to culture. It is designed so as to cater to the needs of specific groups. The alternative schools and centres may be small in size but each centre ensures a more adaptable, democratic, participatory, learner centred and more demand driven system of education. The system developed out of alternative education is proved to be many years' hopeful environment for large number of focus groups with diverse needs from diverse cultures. Alternative schools are designed to address a multiplicity of requirements comprising of different academic options, prevention of dropouts and academic behavioural remediation owing to disciplinary consequences.

Alternative education programmes are meant for students who cannot accomplish the objectives in the conventional classroom. Alternative education programmes are devoid of any conventional rules and regulations, which were used to govern textbooks, class size, grading and curriculum, locus of instruction and teacher qualifications. Some programmes are related to computer learning and distance education. While some developed on the basis of outdoor activities and challenges, others depend upon the conception of community as a classroom or used to merge academic instruction with the work experience of the real world. Hence, we would be able to see the shifting of alternative educational programmes in the form of miniature innovative academic programmes specially meant for socially and academically at-risk students. These approaches are proved to be more personalised and ensures due respect for student, parent and teacher and are found to be more experiential and interest based.

In the present world of challenging changes in education, cultural studies help to provide a curricular framework packed with educational purpose, epistemological principles and the psychological strength in order to reframe the schools successfully, thereby making them truly democratic in nature. As the demographics of our schools change from a white majority to numerical dominance of minority groups, it becomes indispensable for us to incorporate multicultural and critical pedagogy within our schools. The impact of cultural studies in the traditional background seems to be peripheral at the first sight. Bringing in the experience of art, drama, film and other literary devices permits the development of personal and cultural specific meaning. This connection reinforces the postmodern critical pedagogies' contentions regarding the essential requirement to develop multicultural collaborations in support of literacy. Curriculum that is developed to ensure the involvement in the areas of social bonding and relevance makes the subject more engaging and interesting.

Cultural studies serve well as a counter-narrative to official or operational curriculum by introducing current and culturally relevant experience to the lessons. This interjection of creativity is indispensable in engaging at-risk learners, whereas traditional curriculum may tend to control the direction of the transmission of knowledge along a course of cultural reproduction. The cultural studies challenge the hidden curriculum's denial of our need to address the issues of multiculturalism, race identity, power, knowledge ethics and work. Cultural studies are also encountered with the challenge of null curriculum. The null curriculum is comprised of those courses that are not taught because of their infringement on the traditionally accepted content areas like language, mathematics, science and history.

Cultural studies assure a true bottom up approach to curriculum change. This experimental methodology is developed solely to suit the unique needs of the at-risk youth, who are well integrated in alternative schools. The hands of alternative school teachers are not as tied as are those of the teachers in secondary schools, which is built upon the structure of the disciplines. It is justifiable to accommodate cultural studies within the academy as a way to exhibit the values of multiculturalism and modernist thinking. Only by experimentally displaying ability, a society would be able to proceed in a different way by making the connections between knowledge and function. Cultural studies provide the chances to reconstruct not only our schools, but our other social institutions as well, because culture is neither deterministic nor static. The dynamic qualities of cultural studies provide a perfect fit for such content.

The alternative school must be able to provide appropriate training for all students to achieve basic minimum competencies while keeping them engaged in the school. To ensure learning, individualised instruction needs to be executed. Individualisation is considered to be the key to successful instruction because many of the alternative education students are working on a grade level which is different from their grade placement. Some educators theorise that within any single classroom distribution, there may be variability in grade placement as one year for each grade is represented. That is, in a tenth grade classroom, there will be a representation of ten years of grade difference. The reading levels vary from grades two to twelve. In an alternative education setting, this kind of estimation may be an understatement. To approach that group with anything other than individualised plan could create chaos. Third grade readers, no matter how much they have prepared them with sensitivity to their needs, will destroy your lessons, if you are expecting them to read on eighth grade reading level.

At-risk youth are developmentally delayed as well as educationally deficient. The impact of years of substance abuse, truancy and non-participation in learning keeps these students aloof from attaining personal growth in their life. In their peripheral appearance, they seem to be matured but in reality, their social reasoning skills, decision-making skills, and self-esteem stands at the level of that of pre-adolescents. A student centred curriculum proves to be the best to teach and reach students. Using team-teaching approach, the alternative school can concentrate on the needs of the individual primarily and then the content of the curriculum. As with the early adolescent, the challenge of the alternative school is the enhancement of self-esteem of the learners as well as teaching them with innovative and effective methods. Many educationists found that the process of integrated learning has contributed much to the middle school aged and alternative education students. Integration is always comprised of engaging experiences in which students encounter essential content in multiple and meaningful contexts in response to their own inquiry. Integrated learning makes use of the natural curiosity within the students in order to motivate them to learn.

Experiential learning also reinforces relevancy and enriches the learning process. Experiential process, based on direct experience, implies active learning. Learning by doing helps kinaesthetic learners as well as auditory and visual. Many alternative schools in the United States and abroad make use of techniques that are based upon this philosophy. This methodology is particularly effective in the teaching of life skills. Life skills, according to Brown and Mann, are those abilities that includes the self-efficacy, communication skills and problem solving abilities that are critical for the fruitful functioning or adaptive behaviour of the individual.

Relevance continues to be a fundamental issue in an alternative setting. Students benefit from reading about specific content areas and by relating the content area of reading to their topic of interest. Example, a student who is interested in doing agriculture, can read about agriculture and can conduct research about agriculture in order to achieve his/her desired knowledge. Furthermore, all reading exercises which is individualised and directed toward vocational or recreational interest has its own purpose and it helps to improve reading. Mathematics also needs to be imparted using the most highly motivating methods and successful individualised mathematics programmes. The individual work accommodates differences in ability, interest and mathematical knowledge and poses challenges for students coming from heterogeneous classes.

A lot of the fun is included for teachers while developing specific courses to attend the psychological and social needs of these students. Courses in life decisions, health science, psychology, communication, outdoor education, community service, understanding cultural diversity, our environment and conflict resolution could provide the motivation for learners to acquire skills like reading, mathematics, writing and socialisation skills. To call the classes by the same old names is to reinforce the resistance that an alternative education student loves to express.

The curricula offered in alternative education programmes must be academically rigorous, accessible to students and aligned to state standards and accountability systems. The curriculum must be culturally relevant to reflect the backgrounds of the student population and is therefore understandable and meaningful to the students. While the academic programme is standard-based, it should not be standardised. Rather it should be personalised for each student and instruction should be offered in a variety of learning modalities based on student's individual strengths and needs. To ensure a continual drive to success, the delivery must be data driven and real time feedback available for students and teachers.

Strategies of Alternative Education

A programme should be successful when it has a clear focus on academic learning combined with engaging and creative instruction and a culture of high expectations for all students. The knowledge and skills provided must help the students to meet the necessary achievement levels of the next generation. Alternative programmes may choose to deliver the core content through a traditional curriculum with students earning Carnegie units or through a competency based curriculum where students progress via the mastery of the learning standards. Some programmes used in alternative education may be a blended format where assessments can place students with prior knowledge in next level courses. Alternative programmes have opportunities available from students to recover credit and accelerate learning through credit recovery programmes and online course completion opportunities. Low class sizes and small student-teacher ratio allow a more sudden response when a student begins to show signs of failing. Interventions, accommodations, varied learning and instructional strategies can be personalised to keep students engaged and progressing towards completion.

Teachers use diverse effective techniques and instructional strategies to teach students with varied learning needs, interests, background skills and prior knowledge so as to enable them to meet the state standards set for all students. Qualified and experienced teachers do not rely upon everyone, but fits the same old approach. Teachers change their pattern of instruction so that students of diverse ethnic, racial, cultural and language abilities have an equal opportunity to learn through work what is challenging, interesting and related to the real world experiences of each student. Their instruction and teaching strategies reflect their awareness of cultural differences in particular as well as those might have an adverse affect on student learning or behaviour. Teachers of English Language Learning (ELL) students are knowledgeable about language acquisition, how to support ELLs and culture differences in curriculum and in instruction. Teachers working with students with Individual Education Programmes (IEP) are aware of the content of the IEP including accommodations and interventions and implement with fidelity the requirements of the IEP.

Universal Design for learning is a model of content delivery that acknowledges the individuality of all learners and helps teachers adapt the curriculum to maximise the individual success. Alternative education programmes provide ample instructional materials and resources for all students to have full and meaningful chances to attain the standards set at the state and local levels. Instructional materials and supplies are developmentally suitable for all students and attainable to English learners as well as students with disabilities as it includes a range of assistive technology services and devices.

Social Emotional Learning

Social emotional learning is the process through which students and adults acquire and effectively apply the knowledge, attitudes and skills necessary to understand and manage emotions, set and achieve positive goals, feel and show empathy for others, establish and maintain positive relationships and make responsible decisions. Personalised learning makes students and staffs have a good time to identify specific personal/social/emotional and other life skills that need support and further development.

The alternative education programmes embed socio-emotional learning strategies in the classroom and across content learning. Cooperative learning, peer teaching, group formation and other group activities are practised to exercise the development of personal/social/emotional behaviours important to the success of the community. The programme has an acceptable plan to know and address the students or family crises as they arise. Understandings of cultural differences are made to allow for personal success within the learning environment.

Contextual Learning

Contextual learning takes place when teachers are able to present material in a way that students are able to construct meaning based on their own life experience. Contextual learning engages students in academic work applied to a context related to their living conditions, the community they belong to or the work place they attend. Contextual learning can be a driver of college and career readiness for all students. One of the most valuable teaching skills is the ability to capture student's interests and passions and help students to convert them into activities. There are varieties of models and terms to describe contextual learning including project based learning, service learning and work based learning. Each one provides students with experiential learning opportunities that connect academic learning, problem resolution and work place readiness. Skill attainment such as oral and written communication, accepting directions and critic with a positive attitude, motivation and taking initiative and understanding roles, responsibilities and respect in the work place, in the classroom or on a team project are key to students in a college and makes career ready. Alternative education programme offers contextual learning experiences that engage students in ways that will improve attendance, get students back on track, provide credit towards graduation, and prepare students for post secondary success.

Career Development Education

Career development education offers students a framework for gaining knowledge, skills, and experiences necessary to navigate different options available for post secondary success. In a formal Career development programme, programme students participate in a well designed sequence of CDE activities that become gradually deeper and more rigorous that students gain skills and maturity. CDE begins with activities designed to help students understand themselves, their attitudes, beliefs, skills, strengths, weaknesses, interests and goals. Following activities of self-discovery, CDE encircles three formal stages of development; they are Awareness, Exploration and Immersion. Every stage gives a variety of experiences and activities designed to help students to discover a field of interest, go deeper into identifying various jobs within the field, go deeper and discover the needs of the labour market for such positions and ultimately have an experience in the field work based on learning, internships, etc. While this discovery is going on, students will also make the connection between what they do now and future planning and identify the courses necessary for the positions of interests and explore post secondary options including colleges and technical education as required by the job of interest.

Trends in Alternative Education

There are so many trends in education that are directly related to the approaches of teaching and learning, which are used in either traditional or alternative settings. These trends relate most closely to the transactional and transformational orientations.

- *Character education*: Attention is given to the development of the qualities which is being acted as a good humane in society that focuses on more interpersonal and intrapersonal aspects of student development.
- *Cooperative learning*: Group work is better than individual work to attain some matters and qualities. So by working together, students learn more about team working rather than working independently.

- *Developmental education*: Education should focus-based on the developmental stages such as physical, cognitive, emotional and on spiritual development.
- *Experiential learning*: It means learning by merely doing and it can be incorporated into any philosophical approach or a collection of educational practices.
- *Learning styles*: Every student has preferences for using various modes of learning. So it helps them to take the best in their educational carrier.

Functional Literacy

Learning is a continuous process in the life of an individual, as s/he grow, and depends on her/his needs and interests to learn. Therefore, the significance of functional literacy came to be recognised. The term functional literacy can be understand in three educational perspectives.

1. The ability to communicate with each other at the critical thinking level.
2. The ability to develop the quality of life in the field of –development of vocational skills, life improvement, ethics and morality.
3. The ability to learn other subject areas and recognising the significance of lifelong learning.

A person is functionally literate, when s/he has attained the knowledge and skills in reading and writing which permits her/him to get involved in all those activities in which literacy is usually expected in her/his culture or group. This definition, as can be seen is relativistic, for it sets variable standard of literacy in different societies. So what should be termed as functional literacy in a democratic society? It is the skill which leads to the voluntary participation of the individuals in the social and democratic processes. Learners observe a casual relationship between literacy and such characteristics as understanding and cosmopolitanisms. Literacy is essential in obtaining additional information through networks. Actually, learners look up on literacy as a major motivator in the process of advancement and modernisation. This is what has come to be known as the UNESCO view of literacy. The attainment of literacy is an active process of consciousness, not just as the passive attainment of content. The literacy process must increase the consciousness of the learners. There are different types of functional literacy programmes launched for different groups as under.

1. *Functional Literacy for Adult Women*: The Functional Literacy for Adult Women (FLAW) was launched in the year 1975 to 1976. It was the part of the Integrated Child Development Services. It mainly focused the women in the age group of 15 to 45. Here the functional literacy was related to the package of mother and child development services. The content included in this programme are — health and hygiene, food and nutrition, childcare and home management, civic and vocational education. This programme also gives emphasis on the reproductive and the nurturing role of the women, as well as

medical and nutritional support. *Anganvadi* services, under the ICDS programme, provide the provision of functional support for the literacy component.

2. *Farmer's Functional Literacy Project*: The aim of the project is to increase the knowledge and skills of the farmers to increase the productivity of the land and coordinating manageable and timely access to the required agricultural inputs like high yielding varieties, hybrid and exotic seeds which ensure high yields. The project was jointly undertaken by the Ministry of Education and Social Welfare, Ministry of Food and Agriculture and Ministry of Information and Broadcasting. The Farm Radio Broadcasting under the Ministry of Information and Broadcasting, assisted in forming a two way interaction between the farmers and the agricultural technocrats. The organisational structure of the project comprised of an Inter-Ministerial Co-ordination Committee, District Co-ordination Committee, Block and Village level committees.
3. *Rural Functional Literacy Programme*: Rural Functional Literacy Programme (RFLP) was initiated in 1985 to 1986. The aim of the programme is to enhance the individuals in rural areas as they face a lot of difficulties in attaining educational opportunities. There has been a lack of transportation facilities, infrastructure and inadequate staff. Due to the lack of these facilities, they did not facilitate the acquisition of education. The project officers, instructors and supervisors had undergone training in this programme.

School Environment in Alternative Education

School environment should be provided for better functioning of a learning system. It is the psychological and interpersonal environment inside the school and considered as the combination of both physical facilities and academic activities that are rationally expected by the students. It is seen as a major determinant of student behaviour and learning.

Alternative learners are at-risk students so they need a safe and social, emotional, intellectual and physical support from the school. The school culture enhanced positive mutual relationships among learners, respect and support each other, develop communication skills and also they may be active, attentive and express caring attitude to others. The positive school climate fosters the principles of youth development like positive and clear communication of high expectations for learning and behaviour, student's opinions are welcomed in all aspects of the programme, encouraging student responsibility to meet self-identified goals for learning, behaviour modification, guiding others, sharing mentality, contributing members of the learning community, problem-solving capacity and conflict resolution management skills and family engagement.

6

Evaluation in Alternative Education

Evaluation is the systematic process of collecting, analysing and interpreting information to determine the extent to which predetermined aims and goals have been achieved by an individual, programme, organisation or a system (Gronlund & Linn, 1990). Evaluation in the field of education is the process of providing all the stakeholders timely and accurate information regarding the effectiveness and efficacy of the educational processes or systems. Evaluation processes are not an end in themselves rather they are the means of bringing improvement and taking decisions pertaining to the improvement and expansion of educational programmes. They may also aim at improving the performance of individual programmes. They may also aim at improvising the performance of individuals or taking a conclusive decision regarding the promotion or retention of an individual to the next level or choosing the right person for a vacancy in an educational programme or selection of the right candidate for a particular job.

Improvement in educational practice has been directly dependent on improved ability to measure education results. The students, teachers, administrators, society, guidance and counsellors use that. The teachers use information obtained through measurement as the basis for preparation and presentation of learning experiences. Information about student's abilities and past achievements enable the teacher to start at the level of the students and adapt the presentation to their particular capacities. During learning experiences such information enables a teacher to check on the progress of students and modify his teaching accordingly. At the end of learning experiences, information gained through measurement helps the teacher to evaluate student's achievement which is an integral part of education.

As the educational programme is designed to bring about desired changes in student behaviour, the realistic statement of objectives is a must for the success of the evaluation programme. The analysis of educational objectives and the planning of the evaluation programme should be a cooperative undertaking, the cooperation of teachers, pupils and parents to the extent required. The necessary steps in planning an evaluation of the instructional programme are:

- the cooperative development of a realistic list of objectives for the educational programme,
- the analysis of these objectives in terms of changes in student behaviour,

- exploration of the possible techniques and instruments with which it is possible to obtain evidence concerning changes in student behaviour, and
- the selection and development of the actual instruments to be used.

Approaches of Evaluation

Evaluation refers to the act or process of determining the value of something. So evaluation can be done through a number of approaches. These approaches differ in their nature, planning, designing, development, execution and evaluation. These approaches deal with methods of evaluation. Worthen (1910) discussed the major approaches of evaluation.

1. *Performance-objectives Congruence Approach*: This approach of programme evaluation is conceived by Ralph Tayler. He proposed a process in which broad goals or objectives were established or identified, defined in behavioural terms and relevant student's behaviours were measured against this yardstick, using either standardised or evaluator constructed instruments. The outcome was then compared with behavioural objectives to determine the extent to which performance was congruent with expectations. Discrepancies between performance and objectives would obviously call for some remedial action to be taken.
2. *Decision-Management Approaches*: Stufflebeam proposed this approach based on Input-Process-Output evaluation model. Here the evaluator works closely with the programme manager and identifies the decisions the latter must make and collects sufficient information about the relative advantages and disadvantages of each decision to enable the decision maker to make a judgement about the most appropriate alternative in terms of specified criteria. Therefore, the process of evaluation becomes an explicitly shared function dependent on good teamwork between evaluator and decision makers.
3. *Judgment-Oriented Approach:* This is an old and most widely used approach in evaluation. It is purely based on the professional expertise of an expert, who judges the programme. The expert would
   - observe the programme in action,
   - examine its products,
   - collect sufficient information,
   - analyse the collected information and
   - come to a conclusion regarding its efficacy.
4. *Pluralist-Intuitionist Approach*: Here the evaluator is a portrayer of different values and needs of all the individuals and groups served by the programme, weighing and balancing this plurality of judgements and criteria in a largely intuitive fashion. Thus, the best programme is decided by the values and perspectives of the judge.

Perspectives of Evaluation

Evaluation in an alternative education setting is directly related to the material that is taught and is considered to be an integral part of the learning process. The purpose of assessment is to demonstrate competence of the instructional process, outcome and impact of the programme.

1. *Process Evaluation*: The programme is evaluated through observation of actions that happen. It explains and assesses the different components of alternative education programmes like content, methods of teaching-learning and evaluation procedures. The accuracy of these components was assessed through observation, feedback from teachers and students. The evaluator observes teachers' actions and collects feedback and comments from students and finally all these accounts are submitted to teachers or administrators. The way of implementation of alternative education activities are important form of process evaluation. It identifies the gaps between what is done and what is to be done with the intention of providing necessary interventions.
2. *Outcome Evaluation*: It studies the effect of alternative education programmes which have been able to bring about on its students. It tries to explain whether the students attained learning outcomes or not. The entry and exit level progress of the students are evaluated through different interventions. The difference in entry-exit level score is the evidence of the alternative education programme.
3. *Impact Evaluation*: Impact evaluation is the combination of qualitative and quantitative analysis. Impact evaluation focuses on the instructions and services to identify long term benefits or negative impact of the programme. This evaluation programme tries to analyse the unintended or hidden learning outcomes both positive as well as negative and also looks into the sustainability of the programme.

Components of Evaluation

Main components of alternative education programme are listed below.

- *Student Evaluation*: The main focus of the alternative education institutions relies on the strength of each individual those who are enrolled in the institution. The view of every alternative education school is that children and adolescents learn more when they are interested in and are motivated to work on a topic or project. So the evaluation programmes in alternative education institutions should focus into all personality dimensions of a person. Comprehensive evaluation procedures are used with a focus on criterion referenced evaluation. There is also an acute need to see teaching, learning and assessment as a part of the same paradigm, rather than seeing them water tight compartments.

- *Teacher Appraisal*: Student achievement and outcome are based on the quality of teaching. So there is a need for regular teacher performance appraisal. This helps the teachers for meaningful appraisal that encourage professional learning and growth. Teacher appraisal process should be designed to stimulate teacher development and identify the chances for additional support where required. For the professional development of teachers in alternative education system can go a long way in realising their vision and following their philosophies.
- *Programme Evaluation*: Evaluation of academic and support programmes are essential for assessing the improvement of a programme and student's performance. The assessment process should be designed to give information that can be used to analyse whether or not intended outcomes are being achieved and how programmes can be improved. And also give information about the important issues which could make impact on the programme and student learning to alternative education faculty and other decision-makers.

Features of Effective Alternative Education Programme Evaluation

1. Systematic: Evaluation has to be systematic and scientific for collecting and analysing information over a period of time.
2. *Focus on vision and philosophy:* The main focus has to be on the mission statement and the overall philosophy of the alternative education programme or institution.
3. *Formative and Summative*: The evaluation process should be done throughout the programme as well as at the end of the programme for overall effectiveness.
4. *Comprehensive*: The evaluation processes are essential to understand the academic excellence and institutional and administrative factors. So evaluation has to be comprehensive exercise with qualitative and quantitative dimensions.
5. *Pragmatic*: Practical considerations need to be given due importance because overall improvement of the programme is the objective of the alternative education programme.
6. *Suited to internal needs and requirements*: The evaluation programme has to be developed by the internal faculty and administrative heads of the programme which is better to understand the programme efficiency.

Evaluation Tools and Techniques in Alternative Education

Observation: This is the technique, which can infer the mental process of others through observation of their external behaviour. The observer observes the individuals or group under study, inside or outside classroom, without their knowledge.

***Anecdotal Record*:** An anecdotal record consists of a simple factual account of an observed incident. Anecdotes may be written to keep on record unusual incidents and to describe unusual pupils. Unusual incidents are to be recorded even if the pupils involved may be well adjusted individuals. These records may be kept in a folder along with other information, pertinent to evaluating the child's behaviour. In the case of pupils, who seem to be emotionally disturbed, anecdotal records should be used extensively. Anecdotes should be restricted to actual accounts. Care should be taken not to include judgements of the behaviour observed. The entries of the record are to be summarised at suitable intervals so as to have a clear picture of the individual observed. This technique is within the limits of the classroom teacher.

***Portfolio*:** In portfolio, documents of a learner's development over a period of time, particularly important for struggling learners or those new to a discipline, are included. Portfolios are samples of work in a discipline collected over a time. Portfolio may be a folder containing a student's best pieces and the student's evaluation of strengths and weaknesses of pieces. Three types of portfolios are used in alternative education.

i. *Docunment portfolio*: This type is also known as "working" portfolio. Specifically this kind of approach involves a collection of work over time showing growth and improvement reflecting students learning of identified outcomes. This can include everything from brainstorming activities to drafts to finished products. The collection becomes meaningful when specific items are selected out to focus on particular educational experiences or goals. It can include the best and weakest of student work.
ii. *Process portfolio*: This type of portfolio documents the stages of work in a complex project or the development of longer work overtime. They are particularly useful in documenting students overall learning process. It can show how students integrate specific knowledge or skills and progress towards both basic and advanced mastery. Additionally, the process portfolio inevitably emphasises students' reflection upon their learning process, including the use of reflective journals, think logs and related forms of metacognitive processing.
iii. *Showcase Portfolio*: This type of portfolio is best used for summative evaluation of students' mastery of key curriculum outcomes. It should include students' very best work determined through a combination of student and teacher selection. Only completed work should be included. This type is especially compatible with audio-visual artifact development, including photographs, videotapes and electronic records of students' completed work. The showcase portfolio should also include written analysis and reflections by the student upon the decision-making process used to determine which works are included.

Project Based Learning: Project based learning incorporates aspects of both portfolio assessment and performance assessment. In project based learning, the students receive just-in-time instruction in the context of complex, authentic projects rather than in a sequence of teacher telling leading to performance on an assessment. The project provides both the context and the reason for learning, and usually leading to an authentic performance. Stages of work may be documented in a process portfolio, in which opportunities for reflection and self-evaluation are along the way.

***Rubrics*:** Rubric is a coherent set of criteria for students work that includes descriptions of levels of performance quality on the criteria. Rubrics have two major aspects: coherent sets of criteria and descriptions of levels of performance for these criteria

Rubric gives structure to observations of a students work. The descriptions in the rubric avert the rush to judgements that can occur in classroom evaluation situations. Instead of judging the performance, the rubric describes the performance. The resulting quality judgement is based on a rubric and therefore also contains within it a description that can be used for feedback. Rubric can teach as well as evaluate. And it has the potential to help students to develop understanding and skill as well as make dependable judgement about the quality of their own work.

***Check List*:** A check list is a simple laundry list type of device, consisting of a prepared list of items. It is a type of questionnaire in the form of a set of categories for the respondent to check. It is used to record the presence or absence of the phenomenon under study. It is an important tool in gathering facts in educational programmes.

***Rating Scale*:** The rating scale is an instrument used by a teacher or other person in the evaluation of pupil's personality or achievement. Pupil profile charts shows difference in achievement levels graphically. These shows the relative strengths and weaknesses of pupils.

***Cumulative Record*:** These records contain information regarding pupil's attendance, test results, anecdotal records, health data, record of participation in school and extracurricular activities, data about home and family, pupil's interest and objectives. For an effective evaluation programme cumulative record is highly essential as it is a ready-reckoner if maintained properly.

***Performance Assessment*:** Performance assessments are assessment of student's authentic work (work that is relevant in the world outside the classroom) including both products and live performances. It is a form of informal and formative assessment in which the students are supposed to work on an authentic assessment task that measures not just the understanding of concepts and procedures, but the way they apply this understanding in a task which is near to real life.

Classroom Dialogue: Interactive methods of instruction such as question-answer method or dialogue methods can throw a great deal of light on the thought process of the students. Through in one-to-one interaction, the teacher may understand the understanding level and the problem areas of the students.

Test: A test is a procedure in which students are supposed to exhibit certain specific behaviour under certain conditions usually within a specified time frame. Achievement test is designed to assess the achievement with regard to some predetermined objectives. It is designed to measure the effects of a specific programme of instruction or training. It generally represents a terminal evaluation of the individual's status on the completion of an instructional programme or training.

Journals: Journals are generally in the form of a diary or notebook in which students write their spontaneous response and observations about characters, events and incidents, which is general, reflective and introspective. The journals are an important tool for an insight into the inside world of a child and can also be used very effectively for fostering metacognitive skills among students.

Peer Assessment: Here, students are also the part of evaluation process. They also learn how to evaluate others' work, how to be objective in assessing others' work, and so they also come to understand the expectations from their work which can go a long way in improving their own work.

Graphic Organisers: These are the tools to visually represent thoughts, ideas, knowledge, concepts etc. by way of connecting lines. Graphic organisers can be a great tool for evaluation in assessing how students organise and represent knowledge and thereby teachers can diagnose learning difficulties in students. This can be a very effective diagnostic strategy for understanding the students' progress in their understanding of the concepts over a period of time.

Self Assessment: Self assessment is an assessment tool used by students to evaluate the quality of their work, measure their performance with the stated goals and learning objectives, identify the strength and weaknesses in their work and implement revision accordingly. Self assessment practices encourages students to take ownership of their learning, promotes responsibility, independence and may also motivate further learning. It is formed of cultural shift which focuses on the quality of learning, student responsibility and making judgements as a necessary skill to prepare students for problem-solving and lifelong learning.

Formative Evaluation of Alternative Education Curriculum would entail that after each and every step of curriculum development it will be endured that all the principles of curriculum development and pedagogical considerations are taken care of. It will be ensured that the needs, aims and objectives are correct, the content is in accordance with vision, aims and goals of the alternative school. Also that the teaching-learning experiences are in accordance with the vision, philosophy and ideology of the school and they are in consonance with the latest pedagogical and psychological principles. It will be ensured that the principles of assessment and evaluation are followed in the school's evaluation programme and adequate tools and techniques are employed for a comprehensive evaluation of studies.

Summative Evaluation of the Alternative Education Curriculum would ensure that the curriculum is an effective one that fulfils the aims and goals for which it was developed. Summative evaluation of the curriculum should be a comprehensive process wherein it is ensured that the students who are completing the programme possess the skills and competencies required of them and also that the processes followed in the school, both the academic and non-academic or administrative are evaluated. These processes should also be in consensus with the ideology of the school and they should not resort to unethical practices. The impact of the programme is on the lives of students, parents and the community and the society they live. The focus of the programme should be long term. So for an in depth insight of the effectiveness of curriculum should be considered.

7

Teachers of Alternative Education

Alternative schools are designed to assist the pupils, who may disturb the conventional setting with their behavioural problems. In academic areas, these schools are allied with the state curriculum. At this school, the pupils coming from different circumstances are getting a chance for the second time to study in a better way even after getting expelled from the formal school. Therefore, definitely we can say that successful involvement of a teacher is necessary for the successful transition of a student. Students will get maximum support from the teacher through personal interactions. Students studying in the alternative schools always desire to get additional support from their teachers. So, it is necessary to provide appropriate training for the teachers. It is also necessary for the teachers to have faith in their pupils thereby developing an exceptional bond with them. Teachers must be well-equipped with professional training and conferences to educate the students in alternative schools. The training must be focused on various facets of teaching.

Positive support from the teacher depends on agreeable setting and pleasant atmosphere of the classroom. So, the teachers must be provided with specific training which may equip them in managing good classroom setting as well as to assure student's maximum participation in classroom activities. Positive support from the teacher proves to be beneficial for the students in creating a positive attitude towards their experience in school thereby making them more active both academically and socially. In-service training proves to be helpful for the teachers for revising appropriate programmes and strategies meant for alternative students.

Alternative education teachers are found to be adaptive in their methodology of teaching-learning process and to be conscious about the circumstances and requirements of their students. The teachers are ready to listen to their students attentively. They are also ready to hold their students in high expectations by providing maximum encouragements to them. The positive relationship between teacher and the pupil could help the children to possess qualities like self-esteem, competence and self-assurance, which would help them to grow personally. Intrinsic motivation must be provided to the children by the teachers to the maximum. This high level of motivation would help them to believe in their own ability to prosper and improve academically. Self-motivated students would be able to think prior about the disciplinary issues that may come as the after effects of negative behaviours in the classroom.

Increase of a secure and nurturing atmosphere empowers the students to succeed both emotionally and academically. For ensuring their empowerment, individual attention must be provided to them thereby addressing their personal needs and ensuring equality among ethnic and racial groups. Teachers should become a role-model for the students. The teacher should impart thought-provoking and relevant information along with proper monitoring of their academic activities. They should communicate with the students openly and should act immediately when patterns of failure appear. They must maintain proper communication with the parents about the progress and requirements of students. Teacher must be proficient in delivering social skills to the students. Teacher must be trained well enough to restrain negative peer influence and promote positive peer interactions. They should teach them about conflict management. So, a teacher in alternative education must be a good counsellor too, who will be able to give successful interventions in appropriate time.

Alternative teachers spend time and energy for addressing the individual needs of the students along with teaching the prescribed curriculum. Teachers' moral obligation and responsibility towards their profession would help the child to become more virtuous and a good humane at the end of their education.

Teacher Qualifications

There is a special or additional teacher license required for those who teach in alternative education schools. The teachers of alternative education programme have content knowledge in academic subjects they are teaching. And also teachers have good communication ability both in English and their local languages. In addition to this, alternative education teachers must understand the challenges and risk factors faced by the alternative education learners and also believe that every student can succeed in life through this educational programme. Teachers have the ability to change their instructional patterns based on students' ethnic, racial, cultural and linguistic patterns and also provide equal opportunities for all students irrespective of their abilities. Instructional strategies reflect the teacher's awareness of students' cultural differences, in particular those that might have an adverse effect on student learning or behaviour. Students have high expectations from all the teachers that during the whole learning process, their communication should be consistent.

Problems Faced by the Teachers

Teaching in an alternative school is both similar to and different from teaching in formal school. A stranger might see that the smaller classes and less rigid structure make teaching in an alternative setting an easy task. A progressive alternative school teacher knows that this is not true but their attitude is the main factor. Foremost teacher's attitude change is very difficult and it takes a long time to make and requires an enormous amount of guidance and support. That is why workshops, in-service training and continuing education programmes are profoundly more important than pre-service education which traditionally has received the bulk of the resources.

The authority must begin by understanding problems faced by a teacher coming into an alternative school. The main problems are:

1. Problems regarding the philosophy, objectives and procedures of the school.
2. Problems regarding the nature of work.
3. Problems regarding the discipline over pupils.
4. Problems necessitating the provision of individual differences.
5. Problems regarding student motivation.
6. Problems implying teacher community relationships.
7. Problems related to teaching and evaluation.

From literature, it is evident that for teachers in alternative school, there is need for an orientation programme. It is the responsibility of the school authority to organise different programmes for teachers. These types of programmes help the faculty members who face problems in the school and community. Information about the community, school, students, curriculum and instructional methods are the major areas those should be included in the programme.

Alternative school teachers also need in-service training programme to stimulate and furnish the means of professional growth and development of teachers. Well planned and organised programmes not only upgrade the professional competencies of the teacher but also make better the educational programmes of the alternative school. The in-service programme should be based upon a careful identification of the professional needs of the teacher. The content of a suitable in-service programme may differ from one school to another, as it is being based on the priorities of the specific school.

8

Alternative Education at Different Levels

Alternative Education for Out of School Children

"Out of School" shows a meagre level of elementary knowledge and proficiencies and they would not have any certificate which marks it. Hence it may act as an impediment on their way to get placed in good occupation, welfare, protecting themselves from dearth and economic growth at different levels starting from home, then the community and finally at national levels. These kind of problems can be resolved to an extent through:

- Finding remedial measures for the process with the help of alternative education;
- Integrating the students into the labour market with the help of non-formal education and by imparting technical as well as vocational education and training; and
- Retaining of at-risk youth in school. Conversely there happens a less chance for re-entering into the formal education system specifically at the secondary level.

Alternative education, which is also called non-traditional education or educational alternative designates various kinds of methodologies of teaching and learning rather than the traditional methods followed by other public or private schools. These methodologies are applicable to all the pupils of different ages and levels of education. Educational alternatives have emerged out of various reformations in the field of education and hence they are found to be deeply rooted in different philosophies, which are entirely different from mainstream compulsory education. Some are found to have strongly oriented towards political, scholarly or philosophical aspects, while other informal associations of teachers and pupils are found to be dissatisfied with certain aspects of mainstream education.

Alternative education for out of school children has incredible importance. There are three categories of out of school youth. They are:

1. The students who did not have any regular schooling.
2. The drop-out students even before the completion of 12 years of schooling.
3. The students who are out of school after completing secondary stage of schooling.

There are numerous factors of risk behind the emergence of out of school children. Studies show that around 258 million children and youth are still out of school. The number of out of school children seems to be higher in rural areas when compared to urban areas and girls are more in number than boys. Another relevant finding was that the great portion of out of school children is coming from backward communities.

While analysing several reasons behind the failure to ensure the enrolment of students in schools and the increase of their dropout rate from the school points towards the practice of discrimination shown towards the education of girls that is prevalent in India. The socio-economic conditions of the parents seem to be an important reason for the increase in the dropout rate of children. Another important reason seems to be the insufficient awareness. There seems to be several other reasons too.

Both children and youth of out of school populace are offered with many complementary education programmes, which may help them to master basic literacy skills. Two pathways recommended for out of school youth are:

1. Bringing back the out of school populace to formal schooling system or alternative education programmes with the help of remediation programmes.
2. Incorporation of youth into the labour market by developing the work force.

Alternative education programmes are found to be successful for those who had multiple entry and exit points and for those who had close associations with formal education. Ideally speaking, formal schooling is more advantageous for everyone. But in reality, most of the children from disadvantaged backgrounds are facing many challenges and have to overcome different kinds of obstacles for entering the regular school system and later become dropouts even before completing elementary schooling. In Asia and Pacific, most of the countries having high populace and low literacy rate lack the means and sources essential to develop the formal education system accordingly. Hence, it becomes mandatory to provide education through flexible non-formal means in cases where formal educational system is not possible.

Alternative schools and programmes may help one to reconnect with the main stream of education or sometimes the other way round. Some institutions providing alternative education are found to be taking disciplinary action against the children having disciplinary problems and having difficulty in meeting the standards set by testing environments by removing them from the system. At the same time, some alternative education systems help the child to re-establish the lost connection with the society thereby meeting their needs.

There seems to be so many obstacles on the way of accomplishment of education both inside and outside of the school systems. Unintended consequences of inflexible school discipline policies seem to be the most important impediment within the school system. Other barriers being poverty, poor starting of education, stress from the community, racial ethnic and linguistic barriers, insufficient adult supervision, mentors and community supports, family stress and responsibilities, learning disabilities and other related conditions.

Disconnected and out of school children are reported to have no priorities as far as general public is concerned. Alternative education offers an opportunity for out of school children to get reconnected with education..

Alternative Education at University Stage

Alternative education programmes at university stage encompasses a wide variety of models. Early and Middle College high schools, Career Academies, Diploma Plus, College Gateway Programmes, experiential learning environments, and Twilight Academies are just some of the alternative models that school districts and community-based organisations operate, either as charter schools, contract schools, or independently. Many well-established and stable national alternative education programmes are also meant to help the vulnerable youth. Some of the better-known ones include Job Corps, Youth Build, the Center for Employment and Training (CET), and Youth Service and Conservation Corps.

Benefits of Youth-related Programmes

- Educational Attainment
- Grade Repetition
- Higher Order Thinking Skills
- Oral and Interpersonal Communication Skills
- Arts Participation Skills and Knowledge
- Computer Technology Skills
- Research Related Skills

Two important alternative education programmes implemented for youth are:

Work Based Learning

Work Based Learning (WBL) is an educational strategy that delivers students with real-life work experiences where they can apply academic and technical skills thereby developing their vocation. It is a series of educational courses which incorporate the curriculum at school or university level with one's profession in order to create a different learning paradigm. Work based learning intentionally combines the theory with practical and helps to acknowledge the intersection of explicit and implied forms of knowing.

Most WBL programmes are generally university accredited courses, aiming to collaborate the requirements of learners as well as industries for skilled and talented employees. WBL programmes are aimed to bridge the gap between the learning and the doing. "Work based learning" strategies provide career awareness, career exploration opportunities, career planning activities and help the students to attain competencies such as positive work attitudes and other employable skills.

Online Learning

Online learning is the latest and most prevalent form of distance education today. On analysing its influence within the past decade, it has had a major impact on post-secondary education and it becomes more and more demanding day by day.

Benefits of Online Education

- *Flexibility*: Students have the freedom to take decisions regarding their careers and school because they are not supposed to follow a fixed schedule. In a classroom following traditional and conventional system of education, students are not enjoying any kind of power and hence they are forced to work as per the schedule set by others. Most people who choose online platform of learning seem to have other commitments, and prefer the same as it gives them the power to take decisions regarding their delegation of time in accordance with different projects
- *Variety of programmes and courses*: A change from traditional four-year university system to completely online education system and higher education today poses a huge variety of options for students. No matter whether the students opt for any course of study of their choice, say from Nursing to Neuroscience, they can accomplish their wish on online platform. Today, students are able to earn every academic degree on online mode, even from a career certificate to a doctorate.
- *Lower total costs*: Programmes on online platform prove to be a more affordable option than traditional system of education. Though not all online degrees offer less expensive net tuition prices than traditional colleges, associated expenses almost always cost less. Less travelling fare, cost-free online course materials are some of the examples. In addition, many colleges and universities accept credits earned via free massive open online courses (MOOCs), is the most recent advance in online education. These free online courses can help students in fulfilling general education requirements.
- *Career advancement*: Students can complete online courses and even accomplish entire degrees while working, while in-between jobs, or while taking time to raise a family. This academic work will help to explain any discontinuity or gaps in a resume as well. Also, earning a degree proves ambitiousness to prospective employers and a desire to remain informed and prepared for new challenges.
- *Professional development programme*: Higher education professional development trends are increasingly focused on areas of quality

improvement, quality assurance and optimal technology delivery models to achieve academic excellence. World class universities, depending upon their faculty professional development centres for an array of professional development programmes to support teaching, research and student learning.

Alternative Education for Adults

Educating adults is entirely different from that of children, as the adults are in possession of accumulated knowledge and work experience which enhances one's learning experience. Majority of the adult education is voluntary, therefore, generally the participants are self-motivated, unless required to participate, by an employer. Adults are matured and have a strong foundation for learning as they are packed with enough and more life experiences. An adult's readiness to learn is directly proportional to their thirst for knowledge. Their orientation to learning is problem centred rather than subject centred. Their motivation to learn is internal. Adults frequently apply their knowledge in a practical fashion to learn effectively. They must have a genuine expectation that the knowledge they gain will help them further to achieve their goals. For example, during the 1990s, many adults, including mostly office workers were enrolled in computer training courses. These courses were meant to teach the basics about the operating system or specific application software. As the concepts governing the user's interactions with a PC were so new, many people who had been working white-collar jobs for ten years or more, decided to do such training courses, either at their own interest (to gain computer skills in order to earn high pay) or at the request of their managers.

The aim of adult education at college or university level is distinct. In these institutions, the ultimate aim is one's personal growth and development as well as their vocation and career preparedness. Another goal might be to sustain a society which is democratic in nature thereby improving its social structure. A common problem in adult education in the US is the insufficiency of professional development opportunities for adult educators. Most adult educators come from other professions and are not well trained to deal with adult learning issues. Most of the positions available in this field are only part-time without any benefits or stability since they are usually funded by government grants that might last for only a couple of years.

Challenges and Motivating Factors

Adults are entrusted with so many responsibilities that they must maintain equilibrium opposed to the demands of learning. Because of these responsibilities, adults have to face many barriers and challenges while partaking in learning and resuming their education. The barriers can be classified into three groups such as institutional, situational and dispositional. Some of these barriers might include the lack of time in balancing career and family demands, financial background and transportation fare. Others like one's level of confidence, level of interest, lack of information about opportunities for learning, problems in scheduling, entrance requirements and problems with child care could be considered as barriers to learning. Distance or online learning can address some problems with adult education that cause these barriers.

On understanding the factors which motivate adult learners and the barriers which hinder their learning would help us to extend the assistance in enrolling more and more adult learners. Furthermore, when adult learners come to know about the benefits of resuming their education, like the increase in the chances to get promotions or chances to increase the level of one's job performance, they are more likely to be inspired to attend more. A better awareness about the strengths and the needs of an individual learner definitely would help a teacher to develop lessons for them. Adults who are motivated to have confidence and positive self-esteem to a maximum level are more likely to develop into lifelong learners.

In fast-developing countries, the qualifications of the adults are very less as compared to that of young people, and hence no longer match the requirements of a developed economy. This situation paved way for having a strong potential demand for the education and training of adults. These demanding needs are to be met through flexible modes of study which suits well for adults, avenues of access that recognise informal prior learning, and should be supportive to the maximum for the adults with limited formal education to succeed in further learning.

Benefits

- Good Study Skills
- Basic Skills — Reading, Writing, and Mathematics
- Language Skills
- Achievement Motivation
- Academic Self-concept

Adult education encompasses many benefits which have ranges from better health and personal well-being to a greater social inclusion. It is designed in such a way so as to support democratic systems thereby providing greater opportunities for getting better employment. Adult education has been proved to have a constructive impact on the economy.

Adult education programmes are meant for ensuring personal growth, goal fulfilment and socialisation. Chris McAllister's research of semi-structured interviews with older adult learners shows that getting further chances to resume their education helped them to have motivation to communicate with people and to keep themselves mentally active by keeping them engaged themselves. Researchers have documented the social aspects of older adult education. Friendship was described as the most important aspect of adult learning and the classroom as an inevitable thing in the social network. The development of social networks and support are found to be the key motivation for the adult learners. Leona, the editor of the book entitled *Adult Education and Health*, claims that including health education as part of adult education would help to construct a healthier community.

On surveying adult education programmes in Japan, Nojima found that the system of education which focused on enhancing hobbies and other specific recreational activities were found to be the most popular and successful. At the same time, the needed resources also must be provided so that the learners would be able to take advantage of these extracurricular activities. Many studies were done in various parts in UK, which prove the same. It also affords high chances for the adult learners to get socialised.

National Adult Education Programme (NAEP)

The *National Adult Education* Programme was launched on October 2, 1978 with the aim of providing education and upgrading the literacy rate among all illiterate persons, particularly between the age group of 15-35 years. The programme is a joint venture of the central government, state governments, union territory administrations, voluntary agencies, universities, colleges and youth centres.

The education under the NAE programme is a package which envisages:

(i) Imparting literacy skills to the target illiterate population,
(ii) Their functional development, and
(iii) Creation of awareness among them regarding laws and policies of the government for the efficient implementation of the strategy of redistributive justice.

Special emphasis is being rendered for the promotion of education of women, Scheduled Castes and Scheduled Tribes and other weaker sections of society, who encompass the bulk of illiterate population in India.

Rural Functional Literacy Programme (RFLP)

The RFL programme is a sub-programme of the Adult Education Programme sponsored by the central government and executed by the states and union territories. The broad objectives of this program are:

(i) To develop abilities in the learners to read and write, and
(ii) To create awareness among the learners about their rights and duties and the benefits they can draw from various schemes of socio-economic development being implemented by the government.

The RFLP was launched in May 1986 by involving the NSS and other student volunteers in colleges and universities on the principle of "Each One, Teach One". Starting on a modest scale of two lakh volunteers, it went up to 4.50 lakh in 1990 covering over 4.20 lakh learners. The programme has been designed keeping in view the needs and languages of the learners. The government has selected 40 districts to improve the quality of adult education. Only after proper evaluation about the impact of the programme, we would be able to take up in a big way to spread literacy in the minimum possible time.

The process of the Mass Programme of Functional Literacy includes a number of stages. These stages might include:

(a) Selecting master trainers who have to train the student volunteers.
(b) Selecting, motivating and mobilising the student volunteers who are genuinely and sincerely committed to literacy work.
(c) Identifying illiterate persons in the age group between 15-35 who may be staying in the neighbourhood of an educational institution.
(d) Forging a link between the student volunteers and the illiterate persons and assigning an area of operation for each volunteer.
(e) Monitoring of the programme of the student volunteers by senior teachers/headmasters of schools.
(f) Coordination with various development departments/agencies by way of visits of functionaries to the place where the volunteer is imparting literacy.
(g) Telling the learners about the advantages of being literate, making available charts, posters and other materials to the learners.
(h) Identifying genuine difficulties of the learners.
(i) Providing post-literacy activities for the neo-literates through libraries and reading rooms.

Coverage and support by the media and evaluation of the overall impact of the programme through University Departments of Adult and Continuing Education is of vital importance.

National Literacy Mission (NLM)

In accordance with the directives of the National Policy on Education and the implementation strategies envisaged in the Programme of Action, the government formulated a comprehensive programme and constituted National Literacy Mission (NLM) with a view to achieving literacy goals through setting into motion Total Literacy Campaigns (TLCs) all over the country in a phased manner. The NLM was launched in May 1988 to achieve the goal of imparting "functional literacy" to 80 million illiterate persons in the 15-35 age groups by 1995.

Thus, the mission aimed at achieving 80 per cent literacy in 1995 in comparison to 36 per cent in 1981. Involvement of the youth and voluntary agencies in the programme is the aim of NLM. In 1990, there were 513 projects in operation in various states and union territories and now there are 500 voluntary agencies working in the field. In addition, Shramik Vidyapeeths and 16 state resource centres are functioning in various states to cater to the workers education and to give technical resource support to the programme. The TLC phase is to be followed up and strengthened by post-literacy (PL) and continuing education (CE) phases. The NLM while laying emphasis on acquisition of literacy and numeracy skills seeks to create awareness among illiterate people, leading to their empowerment.

Alternative Education for Weaker Sections

Alternative schools, which function well as active educational resource centres, practise keen interest in broadening and deepening the understanding about the need and importance of imparting quality education for all regardless of the difference in socio-economic background of the students.

Education should be made accessible to everyone. The observation about the failure in imparting education to all paved the way to search for an alternative system of education rather than traditionally delivered school education. Non-formal education can be described as an activity that is organised independent of already established formal system of education and designed to cater to the needs of particular clients in order to achieve particular instructional objectives.

The 1972 report "Learning to Be" by Edgar Faure, published by International Commission on Educational Development, helps us to make out a clear distinction or even to think beyond about the difference between formal and non-formal education. It helps us to focus on educational issues that are related with the act of learning rather than the content of teaching in the educational institutions.

Alternative education is non-traditional in method and provides chances to the learners and parents to make a choice of educational approaches available. The programmes range from actual schools to within schools and then to single classrooms. Its evolution started in late 1960s and developed into an educational reform from a few isolated innovations in local communities including millions of students. Far ahead, home schooling and other alternatives also get evolved. Alternative education affords great openings for out of school children, who are at risk and also for those who belong to weaker sections of the society. It ensures quality education at low cost for those students coming from poor economic background. Indian society is well known for its unity in diversity, but it proved to be a failure in imparting quality education. Employment and income seemed to be based on cast and ethnic diversity. Language poses a great challenge for tribal education. Tribal people used to speak in their local dialect and seem to be less versed in the local language of the state of residence. Hence, they find themselves to be alienated when the teachers fail to communicate in their local dialect. Alternative education would prove to be a great solution for all these challenges thereby providing better quality education accessible to all.

9

Alternative Systems of Education

Open University

Obtaining the equality in education and expansion of higher education highlight the need for open universities. This is a great break from the traditional concept of education, because it does not subscribe to the limited concept of educating a person for a limited period of time but conceives of it as a continuing process built on the principle of learning while doing. This will be a radical change from the traditional nature of education, in traditional nature of education focus towards the building of an elite and hierarchical society. But the Open University system ensures an egalitarian social order by providing the learner to learn under a variety of circumstances and conditions on part time basis using variety of media. Now the idea of Open University is popular in the field of higher education. This concept originated in Great Britain in 1971 to provide education to the working youth, the adult population, night-shift workers in industry and agriculture, also persons who needed further education to augment their professional and social efficacy.

The Open University system augments opportunities for higher education, ensures access cost effective and promotes a flexible and innovative system of education. It can cater to the educational needs of the weaker sections of the society. Open University in Britain can provide us a broad framework for establishing a similar university in India. But policies regarding new educational enterprises must be formulated based on our national context. The entire philosophy of Open University in India should be formulated from the context of our socio-cultural needs and aspirations of the people. Then curriculum is framed on the basis of the needs of the learners as well as the needs of the society. The working of an open university depends on the degree of motivation of the adult learners both educated and non-educated. The Open University works outside the orbit of formal education. It is a non-formal system of education and caters to the needs of higher education. It is distance education as well and provided on a part time basis with the application of latest innovations in educational technology.

Objectives of Open University

- To provide adult and social education in large scale and with minimum expenditure
- To stem the tide of admissions in formal universities

- To offer educational facilities to people in their own homes and at their own jobs and at a time convenient to the learners
- To promote national integration
- To advance the culture of the people
- To correct the imbalance in education created by the formal system, the Open University system can be a viable and excellent alternative to the formal system
- It can fulfil the growing needs of manpower and socio-economic requirements of the nation through vocational training
- To increase professional efficacy
- To enable the students to earn while learning
- To advance and disseminate learning and knowledge by a diversity of means including the use of latest communication technology
- To provide instructions in new branches of knowledge related to socio-economic development of the nation.

Then curriculum is framed on the basis of the needs of the learners as well as the needs of the society. It should vary from time to time and place to place. So some points are very important while framing the curriculum for Open University. The points are:

- Give prime attention to rural-oriented vocational courses
- Provision for high degree of compensatory education and remedial teaching to culturally deprived
- Opportunities for self-study and individualised guidance and instructions
- Emphasis on applied researchers at higher levels of learning
- Greater flexibility and diversity in curriculum.

Open Universities are the only way through which the nation can persuade the rising aspirations for education among the people and thereby create an egalitarian social order in the country.

Open Schooling

Many children in developing countries do not receive regular school education. Open schooling began as a way to provide education to children who were without access to schools and the rationale for its provision has developed on the time and the context. This model of school provision spread rapidly as new settlements in sparsely populated areas outpaced the capacity of the local governments to provide schools. Open schooling is a flexible education system that allows learners to learn where and when they want physically away from a school and a teacher. It uses several teaching methods to support learning and has no age restrictions, content of the courses to be taken or number of courses in which students must enrol.

Open schooling as the physical separation of the school level learner from the teacher and the use of non-traditional teaching methodologies and Information and Communication Technologies to bridge the separation and provide education and training. This is not an open/distance schooling for a reason, it may follow different patterns and the learners study specially designed open learning materials at their home or in their work place and they meet the facilitator on a regular basis. This is a system which can be used for youth, who missed out on schooling in their childhood can enrol in courses which will provide them with the equivalence of secondary education without embarrassment of being in classrooms with children much younger than themselves. Young mothers can join secondary level education studying at home. Working adults can enrol one or two courses at a time and also can acquire skill training coupled with academic subjects while self-employed or working as non-skilled labour. Another important point related to open school is that the face-to face sessions with the facilitator are mainly to clarify any difficulties that the students may have experienced when working through the learning materials. These sessions are seldom mandatory. It does not affect the students if they have to drop out for a period of time since they can pick up their studies based on their conveniences.

Principles of Open Schooling

1. Lifelong Learning: Learning is a lifelong process and should directly relate to the life experiences of the individual. For this is to happen, the individual has to appreciate the relevance of what is learned and the motivation to learn is intrinsic.
2. Flexible learning: Learners choose what they want to learn, how they want to learn and when they want to learn. The central pedagogical elements of open learning allow individual differences and individual learning styles and learning performances unlike formal systems of learning.
3. Learner support: Learners should be provided with adequate support to help them achieve academic success. While studying is a personalised experience, support structures and systems should be in place for learners to fall back on whenever they experience difficulties.
4. Cost effectiveness: Open schooling systems should be cost effective but should not compromise on the quality of education they provide.

Open schooling observes the ideals of learner centeredness, lifelong learning, flexibility of learning provisions, removal of barriers to access learning, recognition of prior learning, provision of sound learner support, construction of learning programmes in the expectation that learners can succeed and maintenance of rigorous quality assurance over the design of learning materials and support systems.

National Institute of Open Schooling (NIOS)

In 1979, an open school was established in India as a project of the Central Board of Secondary Education, Delhi. It was upgraded in 1989 with a name of National Open School and renamed it in 2002 as National Institute of Open

Schooling, which is an autonomous institution. It is the largest open schooling system in the world providing alternative schooling. NIOS is created to cater to the educational needs of students who cannot attend regular schools. Students benefiting from this initiative include sport-persons who have to train and travel all through the academic year, those with physical handicap, and those with chronic medical illness and those with learning disorder or other psychiatric conditions. The NIOS offers open vocational education package courses, vocational courses, life enrichment courses, stand-alone vocational subjects as well as vocational subjects in combination with academic subjects. The broad vocational areas comprise subjects ranging from agriculture, computer science and IT, engineering and technology, teacher training to business and commerce as well as health and Para medical courses. The NIOS curriculum can be largely placed in the categories of equivalency or alternative schooling, life skill training as well as training in income generation programmes.

Features of NIOS

- No age limit: there is no upper age limit for registration to courses. The minimum age for enrolling vocational courses is 14 years, for the senior secondary course it is 15, and 18 years for other courses.
- Choice in medium of instruction: Students in NIOS may have to write the examinations in any of the Indian languages.
- Choice of Subjects: Students have the right to choose any subject combination from the subjects offered in the courses of study.
- Combination of academic and vocational subjects: One can choose to study vocational subject alone.

Modular Employable Skills (MES)

Modular employable skills refer to skill development of students. There are a very little opportunities available for out of school youth, existing labour in informal sector. The existing ones are conducting the programmes that are of long term duration. Consequently a new framework for the informal sector has been evolved by the Directorate General of Employment and Training (DGET) under the Ministry of Labour and Employment, to address the above mentioned problems. MES would benefit different target groups like workers seeking certification of their skills acquired informally, workers and ITI graduates seeking skill upgradation; early school dropouts; and the unemployed. The curricula has been developed ranging from agriculture to food processing and banking and accounting. This alternative system allows flexibility in admission to persons with different backgrounds and experience and completion as per one's convenience in pursuing the programme.

Jan Shikshan Sansthans

Jan Shikshan Sansthans (JSS) offer alternative education as part of adult education programme aimed at improving the vocational skill and quality of life of workers and their family members. The programme evolved to respond to the educational and vocational training needs of numerous groups of adult and young people mostly living in urban and industrial areas and for persons who had been migrating from rural to urban settings. The nature of these sansthans has changed. There is a shift in the focus of JSS now from industrial workers in urban areas to the numerous neo-literates and unskilled and unemployed youth throughout the country. The sansthans act as district level resource support agencies especially with regard to organisation of vocational training and skill development programmes for the neo-literates and other target groups of the continuing education scheme.

Actually, the JSS scheme was restricted to urban, semi-urban and industrial areas, now it is extended to all the districts including rural areas.

Distance Education Council (DEC)

Distance Education Council (DEC) is the apex body for Open and Distance Learning, in the world that is responsible for regulating the system. It is a statutory authority deriving its existence from the IGNOU Act, for the promotion and coordination of the Open University and distance education system in the country and maintains its standards. It provides academic guidelines to promote excellence, encourages use of innovative technologies and approaches, enable convergence of all systems and sharing of resources through collaborative networking for accessing sustainable education, skill upgradation and training to all. To strive for coordinated development of learner centric open and distance learning system and ensure high quality of education, meet challenges of access and equity to reach the un-reached, the Distance Education Council.

10

Non Formal Education and Recommendations of National Education Policies

Recommendations of NEP 1986

- This programme assumes that Non Formal Education (NFE) can result in provision of education comparable in quality with formal schooling. Modern technological tools — such as solar packs for provision of power in NFE centres, audio-visual aids, radio-cassette player — are being used to improve the learning environment of NFE centres, and learning material of high quality will be developed taking into account the fact that children who work have several assets on which their education should be built. The essential characteristics of NFE are organisational flexibility, relevance of curriculum, diversity in learning activities to relate them to the learners' needs, and decentralisation of management. Efforts will be made to evolve different models of non-formal education programmes and agencies implementing the programme will be encouraged to evolve and adopt the most suitable model depending upon the requirements of target groups.
- Special features of NFE: In addition to these characteristics, NFE will have certain features which will help in maintenance of quality of the programme. These features include:
  (a) a learner-centred approach with the instructor as a facilitator;
  (b) emphasis on learning rather than teaching, and for this purpose the capability of the children to learn from each other would be highlighted;
  (c) organisation of activities so as to enable learners to progress at their own pace;
  (d) use of efficient techniques to ensure fast pace of learning and provision of proper lighting arrangements at the NFE centres and necessary equipment;
  (e) stress on continuous learner evaluation and establishment of evaluation centres for evaluation and certification of learners;
  (f) in terms of scholastic achievements (particularly language and mathematics), following the norms set in the formal system, both

because of its desirability and because it is essential for the entry into the formal structures;

(g) creation of participatory learning environment and treating the children with the regard they deserve as persons engaged in productive activities;

(h) organisation of joyful extra-curricular activities including singing and dancing, plays and skits, games and sports, excursions etc.;

(i) ensuring that all facilities and incentives given to girls, children of SC/ST, and others in the formal system are made available in the non-formal system as well, in addition to the provision of free textbooks and stationery to all pupils.

- Instructors and their training: The instructor is the most important factor in the implementation of NFE. The criteria for the selection of the instructor would include
  – being local,
  – being already motivated,
  – acceptable to the community,
  – preferably from the weaker sections of society, should have given some evidence of work in the community.
- Keeping in view the importance of enrolment of girls, and also the fact that NFE has the potentiality of developing into a major programme of women's development, wherever possible women will be appointed as instructors.
- Training of non-formal education personnel, particularly the instructors, is the key to the success of the Programme. Initial training as well as recurrent training is crucial. By and large, training days for the instructors would be about 30 days in the first year and about 20 days in the subsequent years. The need for participatory training, based on the experiences of the participants, is now well-recognised. Actualisation of such training will call for considerable planning and investment. A variety of agencies will be involved and help taken of diverse training aids and educational technology, including TV and VCR.
- Supervision administration: In the administrative restructuring, the most important place belongs to the supervisor, on whom depends to a great extent the quality of the programme. The work of supervision may be entrusted to whole-time NFE supervisors with about 20-25 centres under her/his charge or preferably to train local youth.
- Approximately 100 NFE Centres will comprise a project which would be taken up in a compact and contiguous area coterminous, as far as possible, with a CD Block. The main functions at the project level would be:
  (i) to select the supervisors,
  (ii) to generally supervise the programme,

(iii) to promote interagency linkages to give development orientation to the field programme,
(iv) to monitor the programme,
(v) to ensure provision of materials and supplies, etc.

Strengthening is also envisaged at the district and State levels. Wherever possible the administrative and supervisory structure for NFE and adult education will be amalgamated — including the programmes to be taken up through panchayati raj bodies and voluntary agencies.

- Involvement of voluntary agencies and panchayati raj institutions: Several voluntary agencies have in the past, successfully organised NFE programmes. Very often voluntary agencies have bands of committed workers who have the capability to establish rapport with the local community and they can also function with flexibility and dynamism. Several panchayati raj institutions have also shown keen interest in NFE and they have the capability to run such programmes. It is proposed to take positive measures to involve in NFE as many voluntary agencies and panchayati raj institutions as possible, which can suitably take up this programme. It is also proposed to improve the existing administrative arrangements for support to voluntary agencies (VA). Proposals will be examined by a grants- in-aid committee and where a necessary representative of the voluntary agency would be invited for discussion with the Committee. Projects of voluntary agencies will be entertained for a period of 3-4 years. They would be required to send the initial proposals through the State Government but at the subsequent stages the voluntary agencies will directly approach the Ministry for release of grants-in-aid. The State Governments would, of course, be expected to oversee the implementation of voluntary agencies' projects.
- Continuing education: Scope for continuing their education is important for all learners. The strength of the PNFE will depend to a considerable extent on our being able to link the initial programmes of NFE with effective programmes of continuing education. This has several implications for PNFE. (a) Arrangements will be made for testing of children in NFE stream with reference to an equivalent stage in the formal system and specific instructions issued to facilitate lateral entry into the formal system for students of non-formal education stream. (b) Non-formal education centres would insist on children completing education at least up to Class V level, and arrangements of non-formal education up to Class VIII would be provided wherever necessary. Effort would also be made to link non-formal courses with the Open Schools. (c) Scholarships to the needy children, particularly working children, will be provided to enable them to continue education in the formal system. (d) NFE programme would also be linked with the schemes of public libraries, Jana Shikshan Nilayams, etc. (e) Vocational

and technical courses of a wide variety would be provided for children and youth who come out of the non-formal stream.

- Financial pattern and flexibility regarding application: It is proposed that in the Seventh Plan, as in the Sixth Plan, there will be the following components of the non- formal education programme, to be applied in the nine educationally backward States:
  (a) Assistance to State Governments for setting up and running non-formal centres (boys and girls both) on 50:50 basis;
  (b) Assistance to State Governments for setting up and running non-formal education centres exclusively for girls on 90:10 basis;
  (c) Assistance to voluntary agencies for setting up and running non-formal education centres on 100% basis;
  (d) Assistance to academic institutions for taking up innovative projects and research and evaluation activities in the field of non-formal education on 100% basis.

  Even in the educationally advanced states there are several regions and client-groups which call for special support. These include:
  - the hilly tracts,
  - predominantly tribal areas known for educational backwardness,
  - urban slums,
  - projects for education of working children, etc.

It is proposed to extend these schemes to these areas also. Extension of these schemes to other regions and client-groups may also be considered.

Programme for Adult Education

Spread of literacy has been an important programme since independence. Between 1951 and 1981 the percentage of literacy improved from 16.67 per cent to 36.27 per cent. However, in absolute numbers illiterate persons have increased during this period from 300 million to 437 million. Women comprise 57 per cent of the illiterate population and the situation among SC/ST is particularly bad. Adult literacy received special attention during the last ten years, administrative and technical resource structures have been established and voluntary agencies involved in large numbers. However, the situation is characterised by low levels of literacy among persons treated as literate, widespread disuse of literary skills, often resulting in relapse to illiteracy, scanty opportunities for continuing education and access to information. Science, technology and modern research have not been applied to literacy programmes and the youth workers and the masses have remained uninvolved in it.

Policy, Targets and Implications for Strategy

NPE envisages that adult education would be a means for reducing economic, social and gender disparities. The principal aim of the new National Programme of Adult Education (NPAE) is to provide education including literacy, to the population in 15-35 age-group, which numbers about 100 million. Previous experience have brought out that programmes of literacy can become meaningful only when they come along with a package comprising practical information and skills relevant to day-to-day needs of learners. NPAE would, therefore, inter alia, lay emphasis on skill development, and creation of awareness among the learners of the national goals, of development programmes, and for liberation from oppression. NPAE would be a phased time-bound programme, covering approximately 40 million by 1990 and another 60 million by 1995.

Following are the main features of the implementation strategy

(a) Reorganisation of the existing programmes, to introduce flexibility and other measures for greater effectiveness.
(b) Application of science and technology, and pedagogical research for improving the pace and environment of learning.
(c) Establishing linkage between adult education and the developmental programmes.
(d) Launching of mass functional literacy programme.
(e) A multi-dimensional programme of continuing education as the instrument for moving towards a learning society.
(f) Creation of dynamic management structures to cope with the targets envisaged.
(g) A distinct slant in favour of women's equality, and taking of all measures in pursuance of this resolve.

Pre-requisite for the Eradication of Illiteracy

The past programmes had suffered due to excessive dependence on administrative structures, and lack of involvement of the mass organisations, media and the educational institutions. It is proposed to correct the imbalance by taking the following measures:

(a) Active cooperation will be sought from political parties and the mass organisations of workers, peasants, women, youth and students.
(b) Effective support will be provided through mass media.
(c) All development departments will be expected to utilise the adult education programme for the furtherance of their objectives.
(d) The entire educational system will commit itself to this cause.
(e) The district, tehsil and thana level administrative machinery will be involved in NPAE to ensure their support for awareness-oriented adult education programmes.

Reorganisations of the Existing Programmes

The main programme at present is the Rural Functional Literacy Projects (RFLP). In terms of the financial pattern and programme parameters, RFLP has influenced the State Adult Education Programmes (SAEP) as well as the programme of assistance to voluntary agencies. RFLP and SAEPs will be strengthened by: (i) introduction of flexibility in the project structure; (ii) greater use of spoken language of the learners (including the languages spoken by the tribal people); (iii) emphasis on training of functionaries; (iv) decentralisation of the supervisory system; (v) increase in the number of women instructors, even by adjusting the minimum qualifications and making arrangements for their continuing education; (vi) continuity regarding duration of the projects; (vii) application of science and technology for improvement in the environment of the learning centres, greater use of educational technology and research in pedagogy of literacy instructions; and (viii) a direct and continuing linkage between initial literacy instruction and post-literacy and continuing education.

- The involvement of voluntary agencies and social activist groups will be enhanced by creating a relationship of partnership improving the system of initial selection, assurance regarding continuity, simplification of procedures and ensuring that such agencies are able to take up programmes of their choice provided that they are in conformity with the NPE objectives.
- The existing programmes of workers' education would be reviewed and brought in conformity with the Policy directives. The Shramik Vidyapeeths will pay greater attention to rural workers, women workers, child labour and to increase in workers' productivity. The Central Board of Workers Education will take up effective programmes of literacy and workers' education. There will be much greater involvement of trade unions, and they will be encouraged to take up larger programmes.

Adult Education and Development Programmes

Adult education is both a process through which effective delivery mechanisms are created for the deprived sections of society, and a forum through which such sections secure information and understanding regarding the processes of development. Hence, it is of importance that effective linkage is established between adult education and development programmes. Some of the ways in which this will be done are as follows:

(a) Special literacy primers and other reading material will be developed for the beneficiaries of IRDP and NREP to enable them to understand their rights and responsibilities.
(b) Efficacy of ICDS has suffered due to discontinuance of the component of functional literacy of adult women. This programme will be restarted in the form of Functional Literacy of Women (FLOW) which would be an integrated part of ICDS.
(c) The various programmes for development of SC/ST and other educationally backward sections will include a component of literacy and adult education wherever possible.

(d) Programmes of labour welfare will give special attention to literacy and adult education. Employers will be required, if necessary by law, to organise literacy and skill development programmes for all their employees. Welfare Funds for various categories of workers will be used for running literacy and adult education programmes and due attention given in the various schemes for unorganised workers.
(e) Literacy and adult education will also form an important part of the various programmes of women's development.
(f) Starting with 50 NYKs in 1986-87, all Nehru Yuva Kendras will take up in their district one project of 100 functional literacy centres in one block each.

Mass Functional Literacy Programmes

NPE places complete faith in country's youth, teachers and workers and peasants. In conformity with that spirit, it is intended to give a marked slant to NPAE from the present intensive selective activity on a limited scale to a mass programme. Its main features would be as follows:

(a) Literacy work would be taken up by a large number of students as "study service" viz., specific projects taken up as a part of work experience and social/national service, which would be reflected in the students' final result sheets.
(b) Substantial institutional incentive will be provided to universities, colleges, higher secondary/secondary schools for eradication of illiteracy in a well-defined area.
(c) Trade unions, Panchayati Raj agencies and other representative organisations of people will be encouraged to voluntarily take up functional literacy programme for which literacy kits and some organisational expenses would be provided to them.
(d) Encouraging individuals to look upon literacy work as a personal commitment and voluntary service, particularly by women among women, and involvement of voluntary agencies for this purpose.

Continuing Education

Continuing education is an indispensable aspect of the strategy of human resource development and of the goal of creation of a learning society. Continuing education includes post-literacy for neo-literates and school drop-outs for retention of literacy skills, continuation of learning beyond elementary literacy, and application of this learning for improving their living conditions. But continuing education goes beyond post-literacy and its instrumentality including the following:

- Establishment of Jana Shikshan Nilayams (JSN) for clusters of villages, the total population of which may be about 5000. JSNs to be integrated with the programmes of adult education and non-formal education, will be housed in the school building, Panchayat Ghar etc. and provide facilities of library, reading room, charcha mandal, cultural activities and may also include a community TV set.

- Employers, trade unions and the concerned agencies of the Government will organise systematic programmes of workers' education for improving their educational standards and up gradation of their skills with a view to improving productivity, workers' wages and their well-being.
- All post-secondary education institutions — including universities, colleges and polytechnics will be expected to give the same importance to extension work as they do to instruction. Extension programmes would include mass education as well as systematic courses of continuing education for the work force and the professionals. Distance learning techniques will be widely used for this purpose.
- Programmes of book promotion will be taken up on the lines indicated in the Policy. Libraries and reading rooms in educational institutions will be opened to the public in the evenings and necessary additional grants are provided to them for this purpose. Voluntary efforts for establishment of reading rooms and libraries will be encouraged.
- As spelt out in the section of Media and Education Technology, radio, TV and films will be encouraged to subserve the objectives of education and recreation.
- Non-formal programmes of vocational and technical education, based on the needs and interests of learners, will be organised on a large scale, ensuring that women participate in such programmes with men. The existing arrangements provided under schemes such as TRYSEM, Krishi Vigyan Kendras, Farmers' Training Centres, etc., would be supplemented by part-time courses organised by educational and technical institutions.

Technical Resource System

The technical and pedagogic resource support for NPAE will have to be greatly strengthened. The emphasis would be on decentralisation and employment of educational technology for quality improvement. The following specific measures will be taken:

- Greatest attention would be paid to the preparation of good learning materials, teachers' guides, and to training. For this as well as for production of learning materials for post- literacy and continuing education, latest technologies of printing and communication will be employed. The national level organisation for this purpose will be reviewed and suitably reorganised.
- The work of each State Resource Centre will be reviewed. Those not functioning satisfactorily will be improved, and if necessary, shifted

under the auspices of some other organisation. Much more provision will be made for improvement of infrastructure and staff in SRCs.

- District Resource Units (DRU) for adult education and non-formal education will form an integral part of DIETs. In cooperation with other staff of DIET, as well as other resource persons available in the district, the DRUs will take responsibility for initial and continuing education of the field level functionaries. They will also design and oversee the methods employed in evaluation of learners.

Technology Mission of Eradication of Illiteracy

Eradication of Illiteracy will be launched as a Technical and Societal Mission. Such a Mission approach presupposes that we are at the threshold of momentous scientific, technological and pedagogic changes, which may, besides augmenting the range of the communication system, make the process of acquiring literacy quicker and easier. In pursuance of the Mission, effort will be made to: (i) improve the physical environment, power supply and the illumination etc. of the Adult Education Centres; (ii) facilitate and expedite preparation, printing, distribution of topical and relevant learning materials and learning aids on a decentralised basis; (iii) enrich the process of learning with audio- visual materials by enlarging the range of Television and Radio broadcasts and also by developing cheaper and sturdier equipment; (iv) reduce the time-lag between pedagogic research and the assimilation of its results in the teaching-learning processes; and (v) create, inter-active environment between the electronic teaching devices and the learners.

Management of National Programme of Adult Education (NPAE)

The objectives of the management system of NPAE is to ensure effective delivery of the learning inputs to the intended beneficiaries of the programme in the most effective manner, in accordance with the strategies spelt out at Paragraph 2 and thereafter. For this purpose the main considerations in determining the management system will be:

(i) the guiding considerations for planning and management spelt out in NPE;
(ii) need for the centralised policy framework and direction with decentralisation of the planning and implementation process and functional autonomy;
(iii) establishment of effective linkage between development agencies and NPAE;
(iv) securing the commitment of political parties, mass organisations, educational institutions, voluntary agencies, etc.;
(v) delineation of responsibility to enforce operational accountability; and
(vi) ensuring the effective participation of functionaries of NPAE, the intended beneficiaries and the community in planning and day-to-day implementation of the programme at the grassroots level.

Project approach: The critical level in the management of NPAE is the project level. A project may be defined as the administratively viable and functionally autonomous field agency with complete responsibility for eradication of illiteracy and the organisation of continuing education programmes in a compact area. The project will function on the advice of a committee in which representatives of the functionaries, local community, people's organisations and officials of the concerned development departments would be represented. The management functions at the project level would comprise: (i) planning of the programme; (ii) selection and training of supervisors and instructors; (iii) ensuring coordination and cooperation with the various developmental agencies and mass organisations; (iv) provision of supplies and materials; (v) ensuring that the programme is run in accordance with the overall objectives; and (vi) effective evaluation and monitoring.

The operational unit of adult education would continue to be the Adult Education Centre (AEC) organised at the village or mohalla level. The AEC Organiser is envisaged as an activist worker who would run the AEC for organisation of programme as spelt out in Paragraph 2. A cluster of 8 to 10 AECs will be overseen by a supervisor who will be selected from the local area, preferably an experienced and successful AEC organiser. The functions of a supervisor will include organisation of post-literacy and continuing education activities through a Jana Shikshan Nilayam.

All existing Adult Education Projects will be reviewed and reorganised. The basic features and financial norms of all projects, whether funded by the Central Government or the State Government, and run through a governmental agency or a voluntary agency, would be similar, permitting within a range, flexibility and variation to increase effectiveness and to promote innovation.

Planning at the district level: Detailed planning for illiteracy eradication at the district level will be the responsibility of the District Boards of Education (DBE). Technical assistance would be provided to DBE by the District Resource Units. DEB will undertake:

- spatial allocation of responsibility among the various agencies implementing the programme;
- provide overall guidance to DRUs;
- coordinate the Mass Programme;
- Guide and coordinate the adult education programmes undertaken by the employers etc.

State and the National Level: At the State as well as National level there will be a commission headed by the Chief Minister and the Minister of Human Resource Development respectively. Its membership would include senior level political leaders of the main national parties. These will be autonomous bodies and will have responsibility for planning and implementation of NPAE. Their responsibilities will include:

- planning and budgeting for the programme;
- creation of multi-level structures for development of materials and for training of functionaries;
- evaluation, monitoring, concurrent review and research;
- continuing education programmes;
- provision of media support; and
- linkages with other development departments.

The day-to-day financial and administrative powers necessary for implementation of this Programme of Action will be the responsibility of the Executive Committees of the State as well as the National Commissions. The State Executive Committee would be headed by the Chief Secretary, Education Secretary and the national committee by the Union Education Secretary.

MIS: A Management Information System will be instituted to ensure periodic flow of information needed for improvement in management. Measures will also be taken towards careful analysis of the information/data received and feedback. Maximum attention will be paid to the subject of learner evaluation, the purpose being to ensure that all adult learners attain a level in literacy and numeracy which would enable them to continue learning in a self-reliant manner. Learner evaluation will also concern itself with the other components of NPAE — skill development, awareness, etc. A system of programme evaluation will be built into NPAE to ensure that all AEC organisers, supervisors and management personnel concurrently review, in a participatory manner, the progress of the programme. Institutions of higher education and of social science research will be associated with external evaluation — of the process, the quality of the programme, quantitative achievements and the management system. Necessary correctives will be introduced from time to time on the basis of those evaluations

Recommendation of National Education Policy 2020

Adult Education and Lifelong Learning

The opportunity to attain foundational literacy, obtain an education, and pursue a livelihood must be viewed as basic rights of every citizen. Literacy and basic education open up whole new worlds of personal, civic, economic, and lifelong learning opportunities for individuals that enable them to progress personally and professionally. At the level of society and the nation, literacy and basic education are powerful force multipliers which greatly enhance the success of all other developmental efforts. Worldwide data on nations indicate extremely high correlations between literacy rates and per capita GDP.

Meanwhile, being a non-literate member of a community, has innumerable disadvantages, including the inability to carry out basic financial transactions;

compare the quality/quantity of goods purchased against the price charged; fill out forms to apply for jobs, loans, services, etc.; comprehend public circulars and articles in the news media; use conventional and electronic mail to communicate and conduct business; make use of the internet and other technology to improve one's life and profession; comprehend directions and safety directives on the street, on medicines, etc.; help children with their education; be aware of one's basic rights and responsibilities as a citizen of India; appreciate works of literature; and pursue employment in medium or high-productivity sectors that require literacy. The abilities listed here are an illustrative list of outcomes to be achieved through adoption of innovative measures for Adult Education.

Extensive field studies and analyses, both in India and across the world, clearly demonstrate that volunteerism and community involvement and mobilisation are key success factors of adult literacy programmes, in conjunction with political will, organisational structure, proper planning, adequate financial support, and high-quality capacity building of educators and volunteers. Successful literacy programmes result not only in the growth of literacy among adults, but also result in increased demand for education for all children in the community, as well as greater community contribution to positive social change. The National Literacy Mission, when it was launched in 1988, was largely based on the voluntary involvement and support of the people, and resulted in significant increase in national literacy during the period of 1991–2011, including among women, and also initiated dialogue and discussions on pertinent social issues of the day.

Strong and innovative government initiatives for adult education — in particular, to facilitate community involvement and the smooth and beneficial integration of technology — will be affected as soon as possible to expedite this all-important aim of achieving 100% literacy.

First, an outstanding adult education curriculum framework will be developed by a new and well-supported constituent body of the NCERT that is dedicated to adult education, so as to develop synergy with and built upon NCERT's existing expertise in establishing outstanding curricula for literacy, numeracy, basic education, vocational skills, and beyond. The curriculum framework for adult education will include at least five types of programmes, each with clearly defined outcomes:

(a) foundational literacy and numeracy;
(b) critical life skills (including financial literacy, digital literacy, commercial skills, health care and awareness, child care and education, and family welfare;
(c) vocational skills development (with a view towards obtaining local employment);
(d) basic education (including preparatory, middle, and secondary stage equivalency); and

(e) continuing education (including engaging holistic adult education courses in arts, sciences, technology, culture, sports, and recreation, as well as other topics of interest or use to local learners, such as more advanced material on critical life skills).

The framework would keep in mind that adults in many cases will require rather different teaching-learning methods and materials than those designed for children.

Second, suitable infrastructure will be ensured so that all interested adults will have access to adult education and lifelong learning. A key initiative in this direction will be to use schools/ school complexes after school hours and on weekends and public library spaces for adult education courses which will be ICT-equipped when possible and for other community engagement and enrichment activities. The sharing of infrastructure for school, higher, adult, and vocational education, and for other community and volunteer activities, will be critical for ensuring efficient use of both physical and human resources as well as for creating synergy among these five types of education and beyond. For these reasons, Adult Education Centres (AECs) could also be included within other public institutions such as HEIs, vocational training centres, etc.

Third, the instructors/educators will be required to deliver the curriculum framework to mature learners for all five types of adult education as described in the Adult Education Curriculum Framework. These instructors will be trained by the national, state, and district level resource support institutions to organise and lead learning activities at Adult Education Centres, as well as coordinate with volunteer instructors. Qualified community members including from HEIs as part of each HEI's mission to engage with their local communities will be encouraged and welcomed to take a short training course and volunteer, as adult literacy instructors, or to serve as one-on-one volunteer tutors, and will be recognised for their critical service to the nation. States will also work with NGOs and other community organisations to enhance efforts towards literacy and adult education.

Fourth, all efforts will be undertaken to ensure the participation of community members in adult education. Social workers/counsellors travelling through their communities to track and ensure participation of non-enrolled students and dropouts will also be requested, during their travels. They also gather data of parents, adolescents, and others interested in adult education opportunities both as learners and as teachers/tutors. The social workers/counsellors will then connect them with local Adult Education Centres (AECs). Opportunities for adult education will also be widely publicised, through advertisements and announcements and through events and initiatives of NGOs and other local organisations.

Fifth, improving the availability and accessibility of books is essential to inculcating the habit of reading within our communities and educational institutions. This Policy recommends that all communities and educational institutions — schools, colleges, universities and public libraries — will be strengthened and modernised to ensure an adequate supply of books that cater to the needs and interests of all students, including persons with disabilities and other differently-abled persons. The Central and State governments will take steps to ensure that books are made accessible and affordable to all across the country including socio-economically disadvantaged areas as well as those living in rural and remote areas. Both public and private sector agencies/ institutions will devise strategies to improve the quality and attractiveness of books published in all Indian languages. Steps will be taken to enhance online accessibility of library books and further broad basing of digital libraries. For ensuring vibrant libraries in communities and educational institutions, it will be imperative to make available adequate library staff and also devise appropriate career pathways and CPD for them. Other steps will include strengthening of all existing libraries, setting up of rural libraries and reading rooms in disadvantaged regions, making widely available reading material in Indian languages, opening children's libraries and mobile libraries, establishing social book clubs across India and across subjects, and fostering greater collaborations between education institutions and libraries.

Finally, technology will be leveraged to strengthen and even undertake the above initiatives. Quality technology-based options for adult learning such as apps, online courses/modules, satellite based TV channels, online books, and ICT-equipped libraries and Adult Education Centres, etc. will be developed, through government and philanthropic initiatives as well as through crowd sourcing and competitions. In many cases, quality adult education could thereby be conducted in an online or blended mode.

11

Role of Mass Media in Alternative Education

The major purpose of any mass media is to attract the biggest feasible audience through the quality of information, education and entertainment it disseminates. Put succinctly, programming objectives are to widen the range of the listeners, familiarise them with national and international issues and familiarise them with the cultural environment and technological development. For the services to be acceptable, its content must be relevant to the society, it must be related to the lives of the listeners/ viewers and must show a considerable understanding of their desires and dreads, their standard of living and their socio-political and cultural environment. From the above, it is not out of place to say that mass media serves as the most obvious as well as most effective means of spreading information. Its effect is immediate and durable especially in the current trend of world's globalisation. Mass media occupies a forefront position in the task of nation-building. Mass media should therefore be regarded as a national undertaking of the highest remarkable and crucial element for public motivation.

In the venture to achieve the righteous objectives of adult education as stated in the National Policy of Education (2004) and that of the Millennium Development Goals, the necessity to utilise the possibilities of the mass media for effective delivery of adult education cannot be over-emphasised. The mass media are essential ingredients for mobilising strong national political commitment and resources for enhanced basic level popular participation. This is because what separates developed from less developed countries is not gap in resources but a gap in knowledge. Investment in adult education through mass media will enhance its effective delivery (Kigoni,2011). The use of educational media in non-formal education encourages the adoption of inventive approaches in education. Such inventive strategies like individualised instruction, resource based learning, extended interest in problem solving method, learning how to learn, team learning or teaching and so on, cannot be meaningfully and successfully implemented without the ample provision and use of vast range and diversities of educational media.

Mass media has diversities of organs which include radio, television, cinema, newspapers, and Information Communication Technology which has become very energetic instrument to the modern social processes. They widen our knowledge and understanding of the world around us, they help to motivate our individual and group responses to issues. Mass media in society can be summarised as that of information, entertainment, persuasion and education. Let us assess the role of those some of the organs of the mass media playing in translating non-formal education programmes to the mass majority of the population.

Radio

It is one of the major and useful instruments for transmitting non-formal education programmes to the masses. Some qualities make radio a suitable medium for the promotion of basic and functional non-formal education on mass scale. They are:

1. The main benefits offered by this medium is that ability to read and write is not required for one to take advantage of radio.
2. Another advantage of the radio is its availability and affordability. The reasonable price of radio sets and batteries makes it feasible to all groups. People do have access to listening to radio belonging to friends, relations and sets at work places and casual places. The availability of sets also seems to motivate people to listen to programmes that are broadcast. This means that education can be rest secured that their messages are accessible to almost everybody, provided such message are interesting, relevant and transmitted at appropriate time.
3. Radio has the ability to overcome the blockades especially those of distance and time. Its ability to overcome these blockades means that educational messages can reach the whole nation simultaneously.
4. Radio set are not affected by power failure since they can be operated with batteries.

Television

Another media which has the greatest influence is the television due to its magical power of integration of sound with vision. It is a vigorous instrument for communication. Its efficacy in promoting non-formal education programme cannot be understated. Television has been playing an important role in the broadcast of special education programmes for the mass consumption of the population. TV with the presence of motion picture, messages and pictures can facilitate teaching and learning since the viewers have seen the education programmes through a personal monitor (Yahaya, 2003). The use of this media by the providers of non-formal education nationwide will assist in raising the status of the education. Television programmes, by their entertainment or public awareness aimed at educating the people on issues affecting their life and national development could be packaged by the non-formal education providers.

Print Media

Reading and writing skills are necessary to use this media effectively. Still some of the local newspapers use local languages that will encourage the people to enrol in literacy programmes or to further their learning. These newspapers can feature articles among the elites with a focus of mobilising political will for adult education programme. Some agencies in the field of education should engage in partnership with publishing houses, which will make effective utilisation of the newspapers in their educational programme.

Pictures and illustrative drawings can be effectively used in teaching the adults. Graphical and pictorial representations communicate better than alphabets. The print media has a unique place in conscientising people as well as in continuing education. Print media is the cheapest among the mass media and hence very popular all over the world.

Other print materials like posters, bill-boards, pamphlets, hand bills and stickers, expertly designed and produced are also capable of being effectively used in educating alternative learners in certain aspects of their life and deploying them to participate and be involved in educational programmes for improved nation building.

Cinema

This is the important mass communication media. It is feasible in all walks of society, to all ages, from the young ones to aged. Films can work directly on the motions in a more powerful way than any other medium. Combination of drama, sound, colour, music, action and emotion in films exert a strong impact on the audience (Ezwnwilo, 1982).

Folk Arts

Alternative education is also meant for the weaker sections of the society, folk arts from a powerful medium for imparting such education. Numerous folk art forms are prevalent in different parts of the country. They can be used for communicating with local people. Local learners can be encouraged to display their products too. Regional priorities and peculiarities have to be taken into account in choosing art forms to be used. These are more effective than public speeches or corner meetings in conveying messages and depicting desired behaviours.

Information and Communication Technology (ICT)

The greatest potentiality of ICT is its ability to serve as a tool to circulate information and to prompt a contextual change in the life of a man. In education, ICT is remarkable due to its extensive potential in decreasing the percentage of illiteracy, according educational opportunities to people living in extreme remote areas, updating existing knowledge and finally enriching knowledgeable minds. ICT has the power to change the way we practise development throughout the world and how knowledge is diffused to people. Communication technologies of the recent past include satellite-based television, broadcasting and long distance telephone, video cassette recorder and computer-based technologies such as electronic mail system through net. Internet is best described as a network of networks. It links hundreds of academic, government and military and public computer systems together enabling millions of people from multiple cultures to share information and other resources. ICT brought about inevitable changes in the field of education.

Mass media have an important role to play in alternative education. The effectiveness depends on the choice of media and its presentation. The judicious and careful use of mass media is bound to yield better results.

12

Select Alternative Schools

With Special Reference to Kerala

Today various alternative visions of alternative schools have become evident in Kerala. Brief illustrations of some of the early alternative schools are added here.

Kanavu

Kanavu School was established in the year 1991 by Sri K J Baby, a dramatist and writer and it is situated in Cheengode village of Waynad district. Actually Kanav School is a commune, a way of collective living where learning happens at its natural phase and its ideology is far away from a common school ideology. Majority of the students are from tribal families. Most of the children in Kanavu are dropouts due to various reasons and one of the main reasons is the language, their mother tongues ignored by mainstream schools. The school includes the children of different age groups up to 17.

When Kanavu started, it consumed various philosophies in every activity. It did not demarcate curricular and co-curricular knowledge and also have much shared helps while learning takes place. While planning of an alternative, Baby recognised that it was amongst the tribals that collective living still seemed to continue. Modern schooling and society has destroyed elements of fraternity amongst human beings especially tribal people. He felt that probably the best way to enter into the lives of tribal children could be through "thudi" and "kuzhal", their own tribal instruments. Thus, from the very beginning great importance was given to music and other art forms. Life skills are also included in the learning process. Specifically the school has its ability to transact the three R's of the learning process. Introduction in the three R's are imparted in small groups. The language used in reading and writing is Malayalam. However, during the day or within the learning process they converse in the new language that has emerged within the collective due to their living together, great importance is given to awareness of their tribal past and knowledge.

No specific classrooms are there, children learn from every space — in the paddy field, the pottery shed, the library, the kitchen, the cow shed, the kalari hall and also the campus extends to the neighbourhoods, like forest, stream, caves etc. The great importance was given to the learning music, dance, theatre, martial arts, painting etc., which are the notable peculiarities of Kanavu. Each and every child in the school should master a musical instrument. Majority of them practises pottery. After the coaching from Kanavu, the senior students have gone outside the campus to be trained in learning terracotta and sculpture and some of them also learned auto mechanics. Classical dance, kalari payattu, folklore, etc. are included in the syllabus. The main teaching method used in the Kanavu is peer teaching. Every day before going to sleep they evaluate the day's activities.

The elder ones of the Kanavu are staying outside the campus for their studies. They continue to practise activities and skills they learned earlier. These skills have also become a major source of income for the group. The other children from Kanavu demonstrate their skills across the state during religious festivals, school or college campus festivals, arts and sports clubs across the state. These earnings enable Kanavu to partially sustain itself to a large extent. Apart from these stage performances, they produce majority of their food requirements in their own organic farm and sustain themselves by their voluntary contributions or services. There are many ways of looking at this institution, many see it as having adopted a gurukula education pattern and some others see it as a home schooling. As an institution they have adopted the philosophy of education of liberate principle. One really feels that these children are moving towards developing a holistic personality that is sensitive to the issue of wider social life.

Sarang

In 1994, the couple, Gopalkrishnan and Vijayalekshmi started Sarang in Attapadi of Palkad district. Their first student was their son, Gautham, after that a few others joined from close families and neighbourhood children from poor families and dropouts from regular schools. These kids were introduced to each other not as classmates, but as brothers and sisters. This dream school was to be nothing like what traditional schools were, no certificates, no rote learning, no one-size-fits-all curriculum. Instead of starting at black boards, the children set off their learning on a massive canvas. The hands and brains of the children of Sarang came together in all the activities in Sarang. They learned subjects like physics, biology, geography, mathematics, chemistry and environmental science by seeing, feeling and doing. They also learned language, art and culture and they expressed themselves through a medium that they chose and loved most. At present Sarang is facilitating alternate education for children across the country and the world. Physical presences of the students are not necessary. No regular classes happen like conventional schools. Sarang Family conducts regular camps and workshops for parents those who wish to become facilitators of open learning for their children and nudge children to learn out of their own curiosity. The Sarang people said parents who seek alternative education methodology bring their children regularly.

Gothrathalam

The couple, Mini M R and Sudhi Nammayan, started Gothrathalam in 2012 in Ravi Nagar colony at Chavdi, Thiruvanthapuram with an aim to develop the basic education level of the students in their colony. Mini is a native of Wayanad and also student of Kanavu. Kanavu is the inspiration to start Gothrathalam. Ravi Nagar colony belongs to the Vedar community and most of them are daily wagers. Compared to other places, Ravi Nagar is a better place but issues like alcohol, drug abuse and domestic violence are there. The aim of Gothrathalam is to present the hope for a better future for the children belonging to these families. The school would play a part in moulding a generation to be sensitive to their surroundings, in facets of life such as art, music and current affairs and the debatable realm of rights and duties. The mould is designed to help the children help themselves whenever they are alone.

Art and music get a lot of focus in the schools activities and in every session, the students are taught tribal songs from across the country. Theatre artists and other enthusiasts handled sessions in Gothrathalam. The other priority is language learning. The students of Gothrathalam also attended in mainstream school. But they are very poor in their communication; they would not speak up in groups and write nothing in exams. Gothrathalam now plans to make the children aware of the social issues in their surroundings and equip them to tackle it. Gothrathalam people plans to set up a library and have schemes aimed to generate income among women as they struggle most to take care of their children.

Bibliography

Advaita Ashrama (1989). *The complete works of Swami Vivekananda*. Mayavati Memorial Edition (Vol. I–X). Advaita Ashrama: Calcutta.

Alex, M. G. (2014). Kanavu, Kerala: Where Learning Happens. *Learning and Education*, February.

Ambasht, N. K. (1986). "New Development in Primary Education in India." A conceptual paper developed for UNESCO. NCERT, New Delhi.

Ambasht, N. K. (1988). An Operational Definition of NFE. *Journal of Indian Education*, NCERT, Nov.

Aron, L. Y. (2003). *Towards a Typology of Alternative Education Programs: A Compiliation of Elements from Literature*. The Urban Institute, Washigton, DC.

Aron, L. Y. (2006). An Overview of Alternative Education, Urban Institute. Research Gate, March 6, 2006.

Avinashalingam, T. S. (1947). *Educational Philosophy of Swami Vivekananda*. Coimbatore: Sri Ramakrishna Mission Vidyalaya.

Badheka, Gijiubhai (1990). *Diwaswapna — An Educators's Review*, New Delhi, National Book Trust.

Bethke, L. & Baxter, P. (2009). *Alternative Education Filling the gap in emergency and post–conflict situations.* UNESCO: IIEP Publication

Binzhu (2020). Cultural reproduction or Cultural mobility? Unequal education achievement among Chinese college Students. *The Journal of Chinese Sociology*. Vol 6, N-6, May.

Carnie, F. (2003). *Alternatives in Education — A Guide*, Routledge Falmer, London

Castleberry, S., & Enger, J. (1998). *Alternative school Students concepts of success*. NASSP Bulletin, 105-111.

Chernow, B. F. & Genkin, H. (1975). *Teaching and Administering the High School Alternative Education Program*. Parker Publishing Company, Inc. West Nyack, N.Y.

Colley, B. E. (2002). *Alternative schools: A reference handbook*. Santa Barbara, CA: ABC-CLIO, Inc.

Das, Manoj (1999). *Sri Aurobindo on Education*. New Delhi: National Council for Teacher Education

Dewey, John (1937). *Experience and education*. New York: Mc Millan Co

Elmhirst, Leonard (1961). *Rabindranatha Tagore: pioneer in education*. London: John Murray.

Eunjong Ra (2011). *Understanding the role of Economic, Cultural and Social Capital and Habitus in student college choice: An investigation of student, family and school context.* Published Ph.D thesis. University of Michigain.

Ezenwilo, S. N. (1982). The Role of the Mass Media in a literacy campaign. Lagos: Federal Ministry of Education, 80-87.

Freire, P. (1970). *Pedagogy of the oppressed*. New York: Herder and Herder.

Freire, Paulo (1970). *Cultural action for freedom*. Harmondworth: Penguin Books.

Freire, Paulo (1972). *Education for critical consciousness*. London: Shed and Ward.

Gandhi, M. K. (1951). *Basic Education*. Ahmedabad: Navajivan Publishing House.

Gandhi, M. K. (1952). *True Education*. Ahmedabad: Navajivan Publishing House.

Gandhi, M. K. (1962). *The Problem of Education*. Ahmedabad: Navajivan

Gronlund & Linn (1990). *Measurement and Evaluation in Teaching*. Macmillion.

Hartwood, A. R. (1940). *The way of a child — An Introduction to the Work of Rudolf Steiner for Children*. London: Rudolf Steiner Press.

IGNOU (2013). MES-048, Alternative Education: Concept and Evaluation Block 1, 2 and 3. IGNOU, New Delhi.

IGNOU (2013). MES-051, Education: Philosophical and Sociological Perspectives Block 2. IGNOU, New Delhi.

Illich, Ivan (1971). *De-schooling society*. New York: Harper and Row Publishers.

Illich, Ivan (1973). *Tools for conviviality*. New York: Harper and Row Publishers

International Institute for Educational Planning (1997). *Alternative Education strategies for disadvantaged groups, Strategies of education and training for disadvantaged groups*. Paris, UNESCO: IIEP Publications.

International Rescue Committee (2005). Healing Classrooms Initiative: Teacher development for student well-being.

Kapur, R. (2018). Mass Program of Functional Literacy. Research Gate.

Kellmayer, J. (1995). *How to establish an Alternative School*. Corwin Press, Thousand Oaks, California.

Komakech, A. R. (2015). Open Schooling Programme: The answer to education access and quality in Uganda. Paper published in International Conference in Good Governance & Service: Delievery in developing Economics.@4 to @8, August 2015 at Kampala, Uganda.

Krishnamurthy, J. (1953). *Education and the significamce of life*. London: Victor Gollancz.

Krishnamurthy, J. (1974). *Krishnamurthy on education*. New Delhi: Orient Longman.

Krishnamurthy, J. (1975). *Brginnings of learning*. London: Victor Gollncz.

Krishnamurthy, J. (1981). *Letters to the schools*. Volume.1. Madras: Krishnamurthy foundation

Krishanmurthy, J. (2004). *Freedom from the known*. Chennai: Indcom Press.

Kumar, S. P. K & Noushad (2009). *Social Studies in the Classroom Trends & Methods*. Scorpio Publishers and Distributors, Kerala.

Mamidi, R. M. & Ravishankar, (Eds) (1984). *Curriculum Development and Educational Technology*. Sterling Publishers Private Ltd. New Delhi

Mumtaz, J. (Ed). (1995). *The Alternative Education Choices: Private and Public Learning Alternatives and Home schooling*. New York: Soloman Press.

Mintz, J. & R. Soloman & S. Soloman (1994). *The Handbook of Alternative Education*, MacMillan, London.

Mintz, Jerry (1996). *The Handbook of Alternative Education*. New York: Mac Millan

Nair, Aparna (2015). Teaching them to Dream. *The Hindu*.

National Curricular Framework (NCF). 2005. NCERT, New Delhi. Program. Based Review and Assessment: Tools and Techniques for Program Improvement, office of Academic Planning and Assessment. University of Massachusetts, Amherst, OAPA.

NCTE (1998). *Gandhi on Education*. New Delhi: NCTE.

Nicolai, S. (2003). *Education in Emergencies: a toolkit for starting and managing education in emergencies*. London: Save the children

Oyebamiji, M.O. (2012). Role of Mass Media in the delievery of adult education for National Development. *Global Journal of Educational Research.* Vol. 11, No. 1

Perraton, Hilary (1987). *Alternative Routes to Formaal education. Distance Teaching for School equivalency.* A world bank research publication.

Pillai, S. K. (1996). *Measurement & Evaluation.* Kananiketan, Thiruvanathapuram. Publishing House.

Raimer, E. (1971). *School is Dead — An essay on Alternative Education.* Penguin Education Specials.

Rao, V. K. (2005). *Alternative Education.* A.P.H. Publishing Corporation, New Delhi.

Raywid, M. A. (1998). "Alternative Schools: What Makes Them Alternative?" *The Education Digest*, Vol. 54, No. 3.

Raywid, M. A. (1999). "History and Issues of Alternative Schools." *Education Diagest*, May. 64(9), 47-51.

Reeves, Thomas & Okey, James. (1998). *Alternatve assessment for Constructivist Learning.*

Rogers, A-lan (1993). *Non-formal Education: Flexible Schooling or Participatory Education?* Comparative Education Research Centre studies in comparative education: 15, Kluwer Academic Publishers.

Russell, Bertrand (1916). *Principles of social reconstruction.* London: Unwin Paper paperbacks

Russell, Bertrand (1932). *Education and social order.* Unwin Paper paperbacks

Russell, Bertrand (1975). *On education.* Unwin Paper paperbacks

Ruzzi, B. B. & Kraemer, J. (2006). Academic Programmes in Alternative Education: An Overview.

Singh, M (1999). *Companion to Adult Educators.* National Literacy Mission Publication.

Sinha, K. T. (2009). Alternative Education. Divine Books, Delhi.

Sliwka, A. (2009). *Contribution of Alternative Education.* Published in the University of Trier, Germany.

Teacher Plus (2014). Multi-layered Learning: Pallikoodam. Teachers of India.

Thapan, M. (2001). J. Krishnamurti (1895-1986), *Prospects: the quarterly review of comparative education*, Vol. XXXI, No. 2, June p.273-286, Paris, UNESCO: International Bureau of Education.

Van Arsdall, E. J. (1975). *Educational Alternation: A selected study of their application in Latin America.* Published M A thesis. University of Nebrasks.

Vittachi, S. & Rahgaven, N. (2007). *Alternative Schooling in India.* (ed.). New Delhi: Sage Publications.

Woods, P. A. & Woods, G.J. (2009). *Alternative Education for 21st century: Philosophies, Approaches, Visions* (ed). Palgraave Macmillian Publication USA, NY.

Worthen, B. R. (1991). *Program Evaluation. In the International Encyclopedia of Curriculum.* Ed: Arieh Lewy. Pergamon Press. Oxford.

Websites

www.elearningnetwork.io

www.global journalseries.com

www.edu.gov.on.ca

http://www.oecd.org/edu/ceri/40805108

http://www.agragamee.org

http://www.amarjyotirehab.org

http://www.iiepune.org
http://nayeetaleem.org
http://www.peopleproxima.com
http://www.tamana.org
http://www.bgvs.org
http://www.bodh.org
http://www.eklavya.org
http://www.katha.org
http://www.nirantar.org
http://www.pratham.org
http://www.unesco.org
http://www.theirc.org
http://www.doe.in.gov
http://www.accu.or
http:www.teindia.nic.in
http://www.oecd.org
http://newworldofencyclopedia.orghttp://www.summerhillschool.co
https:// www.betterindia.com
http:// www.yourarticlelibrary.com